Twins inhabit a separate world from Singles and view the world through the lens of the Twinship. How can Twins recover as individuals when the co-twin is lost? How can the co-twin be found?

The Tao of Twins

A HEROINE'S JOURNEY

Margery Runyan, PhD, LCSW

BALBOA.PRESS

A DIVISION OF HAY HOUSE

Balboa Press books may be ordered through booksellers or by contacting:

Balboa Press
A Division of Hay House
1663 Liberty Drive
Bloomington, IN 47403
www.balboapress.com
844-682-1282

Because of the dynamic nature of the Internet, any web addresses or links contained in this book may have changed since publication and may no longer be valid. The views expressed in this work are solely those of the author and do not necessarily reflect the views of the publisher, and the publisher hereby disclaims any responsibility for them.

The author of this book does not dispense medical advice or prescribe the use of any technique as a form of treatment for physical, emotional, or medical problems without the advice of a physician, either directly or indirectly. The intent of the author is only to offer information of a general nature to help you in your quest for emotional and spiritual well-being. In the event you use any of the information in this book for yourself, which is your constitutional right, the author and the publisher assume no responsibility for your actions.

Any people depicted in stock imagery provided by Getty Images are models, and such images are being used for illustrative purposes only.
Certain stock imagery © Getty Images.

Print information available on the last page.

ISBN: 978-1-9822-6977-7 (sc)
ISBN: 978-1-9822-6978-4 (e)

Balboa Press rev. date: 08/09/2021

Disclaimers:

Statements about family are strictly my experience and my opinion. They are not designed to harm anyone's sensibilities or reputations. They are simply my truth to the best of my recollection.

All the dreams in the book are written in the original words on first remembrance. Nothing has been changed to make it more palatable or explicable.

Dedication

The lifetime of experience contained in this memoir is lovingly dedicated to my beloved twin sister, Malinda Marlay Runyan, born May 23, 1948, and died July 20, 1987.

Sharing Merit

May suffering ones be suffering free,
And the fear-struck, fearless be.
May the grieving shed all grief,
And may all beings find relief.

May all beings share this merit
That we have thus acquired,
For the acquisition of
All kinds of happiness.

May beings inhabiting space and earth,
Devas and Nagas of might power,
Share this merit of ours.

May they long protect
The Buddha's Dispensation.

Contents

The Quest Begins

The beginning is the birth of the magical child with an adult body and powers beyond even the adult world. In childhood the hero battles with powerful forces, is joined by the helper and is shown the divine sign. She accepts that she will die to her infantile self to become an adult. She is prepared to give her life to something bigger than herself. The heroine prepares herself for the trials ahead using prayer and meditation, thus losing herself to find herself and the god within.

Later come the fall, the descent, confronting physical death, the trials, the quest, the need to cope with the externals of life, and becoming the scapegoat for the fear and guilt of the community. She descends to the underworld to confront darkness and ultimately death, to face the primordial images of the unconscious, and she fulfills her most elementary desire. That desire is to defeat death, to ascend in spirit and rise to heaven where she discovers god. In fact, she discovers that she is a god. Then she returns to bring the wisdom, the magical wand, the lost paradise, back to the rest of humanity. She may be recognized or not because she has transmigrated to a spiritual body. The powers of life shine through the heroine.

The Good Twin: a Jungian fairy tale

Once upon a time in a faraway kingdom lived a handsome king and a beautiful queen who longed for fulfillment. Their wishes were granted with the arrival of perfect twin daughters who looked exactly alike. The twins grew up smart and outgoing. Everywhere they went the people in the kingdom said, 'Look at the miraculous twins.' The twins knew that together they were the most powerful force in the entire kingdom because they were two, which is more than one. The twins were always together dressed alike, and they were beloved by their parents.

As the twins grew older, they began to manifest different personalities. One twin was more outgoing and loved to take risks for excitement. The other twin was quieter and more studious. They had many suitors, and sometimes they switched places because no one in the kingdom could tell them apart.

The quieter twin married a young man who became envious of the Twinship. He tried to convince her that she was the good twin and that her sister was the bad twin. The twin named 'bad' was very sad. The twin named 'good' followed her husband everywhere because she had given him all her power. She followed him onto a small plane in bad weather, and she was killed in an accident on the side of a small mountain. Her husband found other princesses in the kingdom and lived to a ripe old age.

The 'bad' twin was left being bad, and all the kingdom mourned the good twin, sad that the bad twin was the only 'one' left. The bad twin became unbelievably bad because she believed the people who thought that she was bad. She wandered alone through dark forests for many years, rejected in all the towns. No one accepted her grief. No one accepted her love. Her tears flowed profusely and watered the small green plants in the forest. She befriended the foxes and tamed them.

Gradually through her suffering, she began to see the world through new eyes. She traveled into her own self searching for integration and wholeness. She found the lost pieces of her soul in deeper realms of darkness, and she no longer feared the shadow. She saw the narrative of her life as a story, and she began to rewrite the script. She named herself the 'Good Twin' and 'Mercy' and she began to tell her own Truth. She now comes to visit those who are seeking solace and who desire the wisdom she has found on the journey of her long life. She lives there today with an open heart and an open mind. You can find her within your own Self.

Dualities

The theme of warring brothers and even warring twins is extremely common in history and mythology. We are familiar with the legends of Cain and Abel, Jacob and Esau, Romulus and Remus, Richard the Lion-Hearted and John Lackland who succeeded Richard as King of England. For those of us who experienced little conflict in our Twinship, these stories can be painful to hear. Why would one twin turn on the other? The simplest answer is that the subject desires the object which his rival also desires, a process known as mimesis or mimicry. It is not the differences between them but the loss of differences that gives rise to reciprocal violence and chaos. The rivalry is often symbolic, and divinity or succession is the prize. The roles of dominating and dominated, of oppressor and oppressed, are constantly reversed; kingship and exile are alternated. Identity, symmetry and reciprocity are the primary processes. One hero is ultimately sacrificed to protect the community. This one is the scapegoat who carries the sins of all people on his shoulders into exile and death. The unity of the community is restored, and miracles are wrought. Myths, rituals and kinship systems are the first fruits. The loss of the identical twin is cause for celebration because the reciprocal violence is ended, and peace settles over the land.

Is this our human experience as twins? Rivalry is endemic in Twinship, and so twins often find different arenas in which to excel rather than allow the Twinship to deteriorate into outright competition. There are times, however, when we wish that the other twin would disappear so that we could have more freedom, more attention, and more goodies. There are also times when one twin appears as the evil one, the usurper, the magician, and the other manifests as the good child, the cooperative and compliant twin. Then the family or community may wish that the evil one be exiled.

None of these symbolic losses or "little deaths" substitutes for the absolute physical wrenching that occurs within the surviving twin when the co-twin actually dies. Immortal power, divinity, long life, fame and fortune would all be sacrificed in one moment for the return of the Twinship. That is our truth.

I clearly remember the labels that were given to my identical twin Malinda and myself as we were growing up within our family. 'Margery is the angry one and Malinda is the nice one.' 'Margery is the popular one and Malinda is the smart one.' Of course, back then I did not know that words relate to concepts and that concepts live in the mind. Nor did I know that the mind is only one organ of the body and falls under the direct control of the heart, the soul and the larger Self. These early labels, sometimes even "Good Twin and Bad Twin", can have a profound effect on our image until we realize that we have a choice whether to believe them or not.

I once participated in a Modalities teleconference on Clinical Supervision: The Power of the Parallel Process given by Lawrence Shulman EdD, MSW, under the auspices of the National Association of Social Workers. The instructor emphasized the seductive nature of false dualities or, in other words, false dichotomies (divisions or separations). Black/white, good/bad, rich/poor are examples of the infinite number of dualities that pervade our thinking, our family life, and our culture. Dr. Shulman discussed several of them that stubbornly persist within the realm of supervision and client services. I mention them here because these same dualities exist in highly personal realms. Freedom vs. Structure, Support vs. Confrontation, Personal vs. Professional, Process vs. Content, Science vs. Art. Twins are inundated with such comparisons. I treat twins in my practice and am continually surprised at how often the families compare the twins according to dualities. This twin is the smart one; th<u>at</u> twin is the creative one. This twin prefers the mother and that twin the father. This twin is rebellious and that twin compliant.

Then we (the twins) live up or down to these expectations within the family system. I am now on a new crusade to let all of you know that you are EVERYTHING. You are not half of a whole, one end of a continuum, one side of a false dichotomy. BE EVERYTHING YOU CAN BE EVERY SINGLE DAY. BE YOUR TWIN. BE YOURSELF. BE WHOLE.

Dedication

This book is a spiritual and societal journey as seen through the eyes of twins. For all who are fascinated by the twin experience, you will find insights galore into the world of twins. We often say, 'It's a twin thing.' This mysterious reference will take on new meaning after you have read this book, both for twins and the singles in the outside world.

Now I can say to all who read this book that this is a culmination of my life's work. It is written to honor Malinda and to extend a hand to other twins who have lost their twin and find no hope on earth. Only twins can understand the loneliest journey, and only twins can choose to outlive the co-twin in memory and hope. This book is dedicated to all of us who walk the twin walk. Beyond all that, I want the singles to have access to the Twin World so that you can understand and support us.

The most important goal in my life has to do with memorializing Malinda as a twin and using my experiences as a twin to help other twins. I am pulling all my twin resources together for these books. I can share the Twin World with twins, those who love twins, and twin researchers. I have journaled the life stages of twins in relation to my own life experiences so that friends, family, teachers, mentors and companions on the way understand that our life cycle is different, our challenges are different, and our worldview is different.

I began writing this book in the Fall of my life, November 23, 2018, my half-birthday, the fruition of so many possibilities and the narrowing of my focus down to what must be harvested to sustain the symbolic winter ahead. I am the ant, not the grasshopper; I am the turtle, not the hare. The leaves have fallen from their trees. Branches are the areas of knowledge that have grown from the trunk of my inner life. They are long and strong, growing to the purple skies of the spirit, ascending to the spirit world, leaving the earth and matter behind as they reach higher. Their causal bodies carry the karma. The myths of the gods and goddesses within all beings, the pantheism, the expression of the Self in matter, all carry infinity.

I am attuned to synchronicity as a gift of open heartedness. I opened a hand-hewn letter box that holds my prized possessions and found two old weavings that Malinda and I had made on little looms when we were young. These weavings appear as squares in blue and yellow with many ragged edges and missed stitches. They are a metaphor for my life.

I need to disclose during this story that I remember it as I remember it. The truth per Frederick Nietzsche is found in perspectivism. Each person is entitled to a point of view. My clinical work with partners and families has benefited greatly from this understanding. I do not engage in back and forth with clients who remember the truth differently. The truth for each person is valid in the story of his or her life. The meaning is made in the process of bending the experience to fit into the paradigm or worldview of that person, that person's developing sense of self, and the intentions the soul had in coming here. Each client is entitled to his/her point of view, as I am entitled to mine.

Mythology

I am sitting in my fifth-year Latin class with my Latin dictionary and my twin sister beside me, studying Homer's Iliad and Odyssey and Virgil's Aeneid. Aeneas, the wandering Greek hero of the Trojan War, is sailing from Carthage in North Africa while Dido, the queen and his lover, is burning on her funeral pyre, despairing from lost love. My imagination takes flight while Dr. Odis leaps around the classroom waving his arms with excitement. Virgil's Aeneid inspired his love of Italy, his motherland, mythology, and heroism. He teaches the heroes. Perhaps we felt his deep attraction to the Roman world, the Gods of Mount Olympus, the sacred sculpture which I would encounter in the Louvre and the Metropolitan Museum. The ten-year Trojan War illuminated by these classics of literature lays the foundation for the marvelous journeys of its heroes, who ultimately found empires. I had glimpsed the archetypal world that would inspire me to embrace Carl Jung, the great psychiatrist and disciple of Sigmund Freud.

The study of Latin revealed the grandeur of the Roman Empire, the sweep of history, and the depth of a single moment. The photographer Alfred

Stieglitz wrote of a reality so subtle that it becomes more real than its appearance, reminiscent of Plato's essentialism. In art as in life, we strive to arrest the flow of time, fixing an instant for eternity thus to penetrate the superficial to the essence, the universal, the archetype within. 'If I could put time in a bottle' is a prescient song composed by Jim Croce who died young in the crash of a small plane. Malinda and I sang his beautiful love song for him.

The bell rings and the student body flows into the halls of Haddonfield Memorial High School, a New Jersey town near Philadelphia, with no inkling of the future beyond a middle class, white, suburban lifestyle. We have the illusion of safety, security, impending success shrouded by white privilege.

Little did I know that the mythologies and sciences of the ancients would save me. Joseph Campbell, adherent of cross-cultural mythology, its images and symbols, offered me a true intellectual love affair. Ultimately, I embraced Carl Jung who led me to astrology, alchemy, hypnosis, and Tarot. I learned to live a symbolic life. Otherwise, I would be dead.

The Cast of Characters

Edith Hamilton continues to remind the modern world how crucial the traditional wisdom of mythology continues to be. The Gods of Olympus impulsively and cruelly intervene in the lives of men as sport. They rival each other with jealousy, vengeance, and all the seven deadly sins. They have no care for the fate of men, only for increasing their own power. Their plotting behind the scenes is the agent of every downfall. The Fates are their handmaidens and the Harpies and the Furies their deadly arms. Hapless and unrequited love is their favorite game.

I opened Edith Hamilton's Mythology to the House of Atreus, the subject of the plays of Aeschylus in the fifth century, Oresteia. The trilogy is the plays Agamemnon, the Libation Bearers, and the Eumenides. The children of Agamemnon and Clytemnestra were Iphigenia, Orestes, and Electra, part of a Greek family cursed by the Gods of Olympus. Due to bad weather,

Agamemnon had waited to sail with his fleet to conquer Troy and regain the beautiful Helen, his brother's wife who was stolen by Paris, a prince of Troy. The Army was impatient and wanted to make a sacrifice to the gods for good weather. Agamemnon asked his wife Clytemnestra to bring his daughter Iphigenia and then slayed her on the altar. The weather changed and the fleet sailed.

The elders knew that every sin causes more sin and every wrong brings another in its train. Thus, ten years later, returning victorious from the Fall of Troy, Agamemnon faced the consequences of his daughter's murder.

Clytemnestra killed her husband Agamemnon for sacrificing their daughter. Orestes, Iphigenia's brother, spent years wandering, and then returned to kill his mother in revenge. Electra, his other sister, remained faithful to him. Years later, after relentless pursuit by the Furies for matricide, Athena forgave him. In a later Greek myth, written by Euripides in 413 BC, Orestes discovers his sister Iphigenia resurrected and saves her from enslavement as a priestess by the Taurians on the Unfriendly Seas, the Black Sea today.

The story of Jason and the Argonauts who wander in search of the Golden Fleece, immortalized by the Greek authors Apollonius and Euripides, begins with Jason exiled from his birthright in Athens. After wandering unknown and reaching adulthood, he seeks his kingly rights. Jason, his rival, will concede if he can collect the Golden Fleece, the fleece of the ram who saved his forbearers. After many trials on sea, Jason discovers a Colchian princess, Medea, who falls into hopeless love with him. She uses her dark arts to save him and his crew and bears him two sons. When he chooses another bride on their return, she kills his future wife and her own two sons. Jason is the ungrateful hero, and Medea is the icon of vengeance and the dark arts.

The Athenian hero Theseus, a cousin of Hercules, is also immortalized in Greek history and literature. Once again, the hero is in search of his rightful inheritance. He lifts a magic stone to find a sword and shoes left by his father, the king of Athens. With these powers, he rids the land passage to Athens of evil doers; defeats the Centaurs at the city gates; travels with the Argonauts to retrieve the Golden Fleece; kills the Minotaur in Crete's labyrinth with the help of Ariadne; and nurses the aging Oedipus. Oedipus had been exiled from Thebes for the Fate of killing his father and marrying his mother. Theseus meets with ruin when he marries Phaedra, who falls into desire for their son Hippolytus and commits suicide from Hippolytus' rejection. After exiling his son, Theseus learns too late that Hippolytus was blameless. Theseus is a true hero to the Athenians and much larger than earthly life.

Meanwhile, in Thebes, the King Creon has just defeated the Argos and driven them from the city. This story is told in Sophocles' Three Theban Plays: Antigone, Oedipus the King, and Oedipus at Colonus. Oedipus' two sons have killed each other in the battle. Antigone, his daughter, desires to bury her brother from the enemy side, which sacrament Creon has forbidden. The souls who have not been buried cannot be carried by Charon the ferryman across the River Styx unless properly buried, and so they wait in limbo crying for safe passage. Marcel Foucault, the brilliant anti-structuralist and post-Existentialist, praises Antigone's courage and her just, truthful, powerful speech to Creon. Her fate is to be buried alive in a sealed tomb. In mythical terms, Antigone is the heroine who speaks Truth to Power.

Each one has a story

There are challengers:

Jason: John Efroymson who married my twin sister Malinda and accompanied her on the plane in which she was killed. He was rescued without injury after hours waiting on the mountain with her expiring body. He was an elementary school teacher and ultimately a video producer. I have not seen him since a few months after the funeral. He married one of the sisters in the folk and rock group, The Burns Sisters. Malinda worshipped him.

Medea: My sister Catherine, beautiful, intelligent, and dramatic, the acquisitive Taurus. She has two lovely daughters with her first husband. I have only seen them once or twice since Malinda's death. She owns half of the summer cottage from our childhood through my mother's largess.

Clytemnestra: My mother Margery who did not love me as she did her other daughters. Perhaps my colic in infancy was the trigger. I was the projection of her bad Margery and poor Margery. I still have an aversion to her controlling voice. She was a negative mother archetype: demanding, critical, judgmental, ordering me into general submission or risk losing her love. She evoked my free spirit and Malinda's compliance. This submission in Malinda allowed her on that plane in order to follow the others. Mother Margery did take the twins to the library and welcome our friends into our home when we were young. She made sure that we did not approach, know or love our father who had borderline personality disorder and pansexuality. Her approach was divide and conquer; if she could keep the siblings in a state of internal war, she could remain the central force like the sun around which the planets revolve. She was a consummate dissimulator; about money, about alcoholism in the family, about the so-called harm I did to her. I was her shadow projection. I slew her psychically in an act of matricide as Orestes avenges his father. Orestes is forgiven by Athena, and I have forgiven myself.

There are helpers along the path:

Electra: My younger sister Anne who has remained loyal all these years; who has enabled me to return to the cottage which I no longer own; who remembers me on birthdays and holidays. She is nurturing and generous, logical and intellectual. Anne has four planets in Cancer; she loves tradition, memory, and stability. Her ascendant is Leo; she powerfully teaches what she believes. Square to Mars, resisting the domination of patriarchal society, she founded a new systemic discipline in International Relations on women in the world; she taught feminism and wrote books for learners and teachers; she now innovates in political science and prepares doctoral students to make their own mark on society. She laughs and laughs, perhaps a defense against deeper feelings. All siblings could profit from older twin sisters who set a high mark.

Theseus: Her husband Al who always accepted me as I am; who canoed the Delaware River in my young adulthood with Bob, me, Malinda and John; who wanted to be a Jesuit priest and changed his mind; who has nurtured and warmed Annie through all her achievements; who like any good Canadian loves to curl. He is the best golfer, the oldest brother, larger than life, loyal to his brothers and sister, loyal to my mother and father, and ultimately loyal to me.

I myself am Iphigenia, among other heroines. Her father sacrifices Iphigenia to the Gods to ensure good weather for their assault on Troy. After her sacrifice she becomes a priestess in the afterlife.

Who was Malinda?

Malinda at 39 was a strong feminist, a dedicated educator, an excellent tennis player. Her loyalty to the Twinship was solid as the rocks on which we played. She was elemental: Earth, Air, Fire, Water.

In high school I was a little stronger or perhaps more aggressive; I played tier one in tennis singles and she played tier two. In basketball she was a guard, and I was a rover who could play at both ends. My shooting was terrible, but I could run and dribble. Malinda and I loved sports and both of us played well. We ran like the wind in field hockey. I was a right wing and she was a half-back.

Malinda was more compliant and kinder than I. In Ithaca during her 30s, she loved her anchor role on *More Than the News*. Her production group became Democratic Socialists, and their self-produced program propelled them into the public eye. It seems that we all moved to the Left as our life experiences mounted.

Malinda taught elementary school, Learning Disabilities, special needs classes, and briefly French. Her husband John was also an elementary school teacher. They moved from Northern Virginia to Washington DC and finally Ithaca, NY where they could assuredly find work simultaneously in any new school system. She loved her students and they absolutely adored her. She had a special way of smiling, dressing, and listening that made her beloved.

Malinda was slender, gracious with long brunette hair to her waist. My mother called her 'my perfect 10.' She and John wanted a child, but it did not happen. Malinda was unwilling to go as far as IVF. Identical twins often find that both are infertile. I do not know the medical explanation for this, but it was true for us. She laughed and told everyone that she was 'child free.'

Malinda's point of view on life was only one degree to the left of mine. Malinda loved being a twin. We started separating most acutely when she married John. The husbands of twins often do not appreciate the co-twin due to conflicting loyalties, but John truly believed that I was unkind. This was my 'Dakini' period when, after rape, all the rage came pouring out. I was emotionally challenged. I could not find a way to help myself or her. Twins do grow apart in such cases.

Marrying Twins

I must discuss my marriages because the patterns are so synchronous. I married to reproduce the Twinship.

I met Bob Gorman, a fellow VISTA volunteer, in Philadelphia. He had just graduated from law school and during VISTA worked for the Lawyers' Committee for Civil Rights. Frank Rizzo, the infamous police commissioner, certainly granted no rights to the black populations in West and South Philadelphia. How did I know that Bob was a fraternal twin with a sister Bonnie? After the initial attraction, I discovered this salient fact. We were married for eight years until I was brutally raped at 24; this event destroyed the bond. He married a mutual friend Karen and had two children with her. I never saw him again after he left the condominium to live with Karen. I saw her at a professional event before Hank and I left for Colorado and she was kind to me.

Hank Walker was my second husband for 13 years. We looked like twins and were both born in Gemini, one year apart. My date of birth was 5/23/1948 and his was 5/27/1947. We had been lovers for eight years while I was married to Bob Gorman and then Hank left for Colorado to work at Denver International Airport. Out of the blue, he called me in 1992. We were thrilled to be together and loved our life. We shared pervasive common interests and wonderful sexual chemistry. We were terrific companions. He moved into the condo in Harmon Cove where we lived for many years. When I retired in 2000, we built the beautiful Durango, CO house together.

We chose a day to be married in a small private ceremony with just the two of us; Malinda had married John on the same day, October 14. My mother reminded me of this synchronistic date. I did not realize. We eventually divorced in November of 2006 after 13 years of marriage. My other twin soul Hank was also destined to join her in early death. His alcoholism was so acute, with severe binges every three months like clockwork. I could no longer bear the stress. In Durango, I got a restraining order because he still pursued me across time and space. He remained in Bonita Springs, Florida near his aunts, his father's sisters, sober but badly diseased from his self-destruction. At 62, after several years sober with AA, he died from heart failure while riding his bike. Anne, my sister and I had visited him a year before, and he was badly disfigured, stooped, swollen, toothless. To think that a pro-football player and hugely powerful man could be taken down by alcoholism. His mother wrote to me of his death after I called to say I could not reach him. I circled back into despair. Everyone I love leaves me.

My current companion, Dennis Hartigan, is also a fraternal twin. His brother Barry suicided by hanging, and so Dennis and I decided to 'twin up.' We four twins had attended Haddonfield Memorial High School together from 1962 to 1966 in Haddonfield, New Jersey, outside Philadelphia. 40+ years later, we reunited. We are the same age and have cohabitated very happily for 8 years. Dennis' grief is still acute, whereas my grief is attenuated after 33 years. He has learned to live into the future. He most desires a relationship with his four children.

The narrative follows in subsequent chapters. Karma is the judge.

The Tao is the One

The Tao is the One.

The Two is the Yin and the Yang.
The three are Heaven, Humanity, and Earth. The
Tao is the harmony of Heaven and Earth.
The dark is the root of the light. The still is the source of all motion.
The wise one trusts her heart above all; she lets all
things come and go and focuses on Heaven.
It is beyond 'is' and 'is not.' How do I know this is true?
I look inside myself and see.
She who is centered in the Tao can go where she wishes without danger.
She perceives universal harmony, even amidst great
pain, because she has found peace in her heart.

Adapted from Lao Tzu, Tao Te Ching

Lao Tzu was the keeper of imperial archives in the province of Honan in the 6th Century BC. He recognized the Tao and glorified it in the Tao Te Ching. Then he disappeared. The Tao is the Way, the eternal harmony of Heaven and Earth, the way water flows. The way of the Tao underlies all things. Human action harmonious with the Tao is spontaneous, effortless, inexhaustible.

The perfected individual is a sage free from desire and strife. How does one recognize the Tao? Through stillness. Through observation. Through non-resistance.

How would twins find their path? We occupy a separate world from the individual. The Twin World. We do not see what others see and they do not see what we see. Our lenses of perception are different. We know two-ness, unconditional love, the mirrored Self. Four eyes see what two cannot.

I AM an Identical Twin. This fact of my life on Earth occupies the center of my soul and Myself. All else flows from it as the Tao flows as one with the current. The Tao, the Way, I have chosen for this incarnation on Earth is informed by the knowledge that I was blessed with two lives originating from one set of possibilities. Two alternate realities arising from one singular event, one moment in the delusion of linear time. A choice? A destiny? In the eternal cycle, a choice point arrived, and my sister Malinda and I took the road less traveled. Our Atman, our eternal souls, chose Twinship. And that indeed has made all the difference.

The Tao of Twins is a way to live that is ingrained in nature. We twins live in the Twin World. Few penetrate the boundaries of this rarefied universe. For us, the path is clear; the Twinship is the alpha and omega; the journey is four feet on one path and four hands on one task; the loyalty remains always to the twin.

The Heroine Journey

Joseph Campbell: The heroine ventures forth from the world of common day into a world of supernatural wonder. Fabulous forces are encountered there, and a decisive victory is won. But only through the heroine's great losses does the victory come into focus. The heroine comes back from this mysterious adventure with the power to bestow boons on her community.

The Heroine's Journey is the life work of all persons who aspire to self-actualization, to serve others and to ascend spiritually. So easy to say and a lifetime to achieve.

The mythologists of the modern era, CG Jung, J Campbell, DA Leeming, E Hamilton, Sir J Frazier, R Graves, and C Levi-Strauss, to name a very few, agree that through diffusion or parallelism cultures have coincided in the stories and rituals of the hero monomyth. This monomyth is the primordial image of the unconscious. The hero is the man or woman who has battled past personal limitations to achieve valid human forms. The soul's high adventure requires losing the personal self to find the all-inclusive Self in the pattern of the cosmos. It is the eternal light of universal consciousness.

The heroine's journey is a journey inward to recover the soul and manifest her own myth. The sacred space of creative incubation allows her to know who she is and who she is becoming. The myth is her song. Following this mythical journey, she accepts the burden of her life, experiencing suffering, finding wisdom and being initiated into the higher realms. Inside she finds the transcendent function to allow such ascension. Is the hero going to split into higher and lower functions? She learns to hold them together. She achieves non-duality. She becomes whole. She learns to live 'in the world but not of the world.' She rises above space and time and brings her inner peace into the world. Others respond with love and the bushes flower.

In *Thus Spoke Zarathustra*, Nietzsche describes the young person as the camel who takes instruction with obedience and becomes loaded down by family and society. This camel transforms to a lion who must kill the dragon, the 'thou shalt' culture, and then transforms to the innocence of a child. The wheel rolls out of its own center, the mandala, embracing what one has learned. Stay at the center while the wheel of fortune turns. Remain in full consciousness, beingness, Sat Chit Ananda.

In the mythological paradigm of the Greek and Roman worlds, seven divine feminine archetypes support the heroine's journey. Each woman who walks this walk finds these archetypal images in herself. All heroines draw upon their power. They are symbolic expressions of the infinite possibilities in quantum reality. The post-modern masculine is not as powerful and easily exhausted through aggression or violence.

Demeter is the mother, the goddess of fertility and the seasons.

Athena is wisdom, art, culture and science.

Artemis or Diana is nature.

Aphrodite or Venus is beauty and romantic love.

Hera is power and speaks truth to power.

Persephone is healing, alchemy, magic, the shadow.

Hestia is the homemaker, home and hearth.

Alchemy

In Jungian terms, the journey is also an alchemical process. It begins with the Philosopher's Stone or *prima matera* and then evolves spiritually through a variety of operations to turn dross to gold. Clearly the evolution of the psyche throughout the life cycle is replete with alchemical interactions that change us irreversibly. We recognize them in transitions, traumas, rites of passage, dreams, birth and death. Their symbols haunt our dreams.

In this story of twin loss and recovery, the *coagulation* is the beginning.

Then come objects falling, planes crashing, grounding, facing reality, courage, endurance, making choices and manifesting them on Earth. Saturn is the harsh patriarch, and his presence signals frustration, guilt and depression. He contracts the world in moments of choosing and acting. Indeed, the moment of Malinda's death was such a catalyst for me and forced me to choose between life on earth or death to join her.

The *mortification* follows. Something dies: a person, a way of life, a phase, a dream, an identity or all of this. The pain is enormous. The intention is to grieve.

Transitio: bridges, doorways, the shore, beaches, porches, boundaries and borders. We have reached the edge of one world and face confusion, disorientation, fear, anxiety, and loss.

Putrefactio: the intent to identify what is rotten, then discard. The feelings are fatigue, sluggishness, melancholy, discontent, emptiness, isolation, bitterness.

Calcinatio is the refiner's fire where we are purged of grosser desires and forced to examine what we truly value. Disillusionment. Pluto, the power of life and death, is the ruler of the manifest.

Separatio: sorting, classifying, separating, discriminating. With coolness or detachment, the intent to clearly differentiate what is staying and what is going. Mars, metal, rational.

Solutio: dissolving, structural entropy, go with the flow. Do not resist dissolution, reflection, reflective surfaces, or mirrors. Neptune is the water sign, submerge and surrender to the collective mind.

Sublimatio: new direction, rising above situations to see from a higher perspective, upward movement, high peaks and mountains, Jupiter and Uranus, air above the clouds.

I AM ABSOLUTELY CLEAR THAT I HAVE ENDURED ALL THIS. Have I become Gold?

Cosmology of Twins

In the modern world, we have a paucity of symbols, and so I have set out to explore the psyche for more of them. My quest is to find the symbols that will define Twinship and illuminate the reasons for my life and for her death.

Castor and Pollux from Roman mythology are the incarnation of Twinship in the starry heavens as the constellation Gemini. Malinda and I were born under that constellation on May 23, 1948. Gemini is our sun sign and Scorpio is our rising sign. The myth tells the story of two brothers, one of whom is granted immortality by Zeus while the other remains mortal. He sentences them to forever apartness, so that one will live during daylight and the other after nightfall. They beg Zeus to allow them to spend their destinies together. He relents and puts them both in the sky together as the constellation Gemini, the Twins.

Helen of Troy, the most beautiful woman in the world according to Paris, was twins with Clytemnestra. One myth tells that all four including Castor and Pollux were born from Leda and Zeus, when Zeus was disguised as a Swan. With mythological parenting mixed between mortal and immortal, the archetype of the twin is elaborated by this dual nature.

Cosmology of the Navajo Twins: In Dine creation myths, the Hero Twins story takes place at the emergence of the Fourth World, at a time when humans as we know them now were just beginning to inhabit the world. The young adolescent Hero Twins at the center of this story are born of a union between Changing Woman, the first woman, and their estranged father, the Sun. Against their mother's wishes, the boys wander far from the family hogan in search of their father.

Seeing their mother unguarded, Yé'iitsoh, the most fearsome of the monstrous beasts, threatens Changing Woman, vowing to devour her sons. Deeply ashamed, the boys set off across the desert to find a way to help their people and protect their mother. Riding atop a holy rainbow, they are delivered to Spider Woman. The female deity gives them a hoop made from feathers of monster eagles and teaches them powerful songs to ward off enemies. Soon, boulders attempt to crush the twins, reeds try to slash them, cactuses seek to pierce them with their spines, and boiling sand dunes do their best to shrivel them to ashes. But they must first win their father's approval, who distrusts the twins as potential enemies and doubts his blood ties to them.

With their songs and hoops, the twins fend off the natural forces. The twins make their way to their father, the Sun, who will bestow supernatural tools -- armor made of flint and arrows made of lightning -- to vanquish Yé'iitsoh.

Aristophanes relates that man was once huge with four arms and four legs. Zeus is annoyed by man's hubris and cuts him in half. Thus, humans seek their other half.

Twinship is more important for twins than identification with the individual self. The master status of Twin gives us our primary identification in a world filled with singles. In terms of society, we are a privileged class. We know that we are special, that we are unique, that we attract attention, and that we have powers. In fact, we live in a Twin World. The only people who are allowed in that world are Twins. They are the only people who truly understand us and share in our worldview.

The lack of understanding of twins has its pitfalls. We are not the same as you, and therefore we cannot trust that you will guide us properly. Many of you think that we are singles who happen to look like each other or to accidentally have been born together. We often masquerade as singles in the eyes of society. If you scratch the surface, however, you will always encounter a Twin.

Our true loyalties always lie in the Twin World.

Inside the Twin World, we frankly do not need much from the outside world. In that world, we receive recognition, validation, belongingness, self-reflection and mirroring. When my friend Trudy would reunite with her sister Judy, they would say 'we are all here now.' Our favorite saying is 'It's a Twin Thing.' We know that you will not understand us, and this is a truth of our lives. We live in a world that individuals, or singles as we call you, will never penetrate. We live in Magic. We are powerful, miraculous, whole, special, and loved by each other in a way that no one can grasp. We know that we have a love that is deeper than all other loves on Earth. We just know this.

We also know that singles do not see the world as we see it. We feel their aloneness, their individuality, their singularity and we have sympathy for them that they are not Twins. Sometimes we imagine that they are lonely, that they lack playmates, that they have no one with whom to share intimate secrets, that they are frail in the face of such a harsh world.

The Buddhists say that one of their heavens is made up of only Twins, thus Twinship is a much-evolved state of spiritual attainment. We know that we have been rewarded immensely for some past deed, perhaps good karma from eons ago. We recognize that we are fortunate and that most other people wish to be twins.

We are ready for all the questions. What is it like to be a twin? How do you differ from singles? Are you identical or fraternal? Which one was born first? Did you have the same classes? Could the teachers tell you apart? Did you confuse your boyfriends? Could you do mental telepathy? Did she take your tests? Did you wear the same clothes?

We know that we are the epitome of dualism. The paradox of two being one is our life journey. How can we explain that we are the same and yet different? We are the yin and the yang, the juxtaposition of time and eternity. We are both the ego and the immortal soul combined, and these roles are interchangeable. We believe that we have both mortal and immortal aspects, that one will carry the other past the grave, and that we will never be separated by death. Wolfgang Pauli discusses the black and white keys on the piano: the melody requires both. The dualism of quantity and quality, science and inherent meaning, secular and sacred, mortal and immortal, are incarnated in us. How can any life have more relevance to the wholeness and oneness of the universe?

The quantum world within mathematics and physics has opened our minds to the relativity of time and space, the oneness of the universal consciousness, the *Conjunctio* and *Dissolutio* within alchemy. This quantum revelation assigns to the universal field all possibilities, solely energy, non-local correlations, entanglement, leaps of creativity and imagination, the embrace of uncertainty, and subject-object collapse. The Unified Field of Consciousness -Chita Shakti- has been discovered at last by science.

Spirituality and religion have recognized this truth since the dawn of creation. It is the Big Bang, the Word made Flesh, Vishnu's dream. The wave and the particle are indivisible.

Numerology is omnipresent in the twin psyches. The one becomes the two, becomes the three and becomes the 10,000 things in the Tao. In Buddhism, the 10,000 joys and the 10,000 sorrows illustrate the growing complexity of matter as manifested from spirit. The universe proliferates and expands at a speed faster than light. As twins, we hold the archetypal position of Two. The Three position is the trinity within all major religions: Christian (God, Son and Holy Spirit), Hindu (Brahma, Shiva and Vishnu); Buddhism (Buddha, Sangha and Dharma); Tao (Heaven, Earth and Wu Ji).

What are the twins teaching me? Instead of I, we. We do. We are. Us, not me. Look at us.

Twins have secret languages and magical names for each other. We refer to each other as Twin, 'Twinnie', Sis, Sister, rather than our given names.

Twins are feral; we raise ourselves. Mothers and fathers cannot penetrate our bonds. It is a twin thing; you would not understand. You are not a twin. We are special.

What does Twinship mean? There is no real I. Twin attachment is the only secure one. The mother is an outsider.

The bond can become a burden. Eliade presents *The God who Binds* and the *Symbolism of Knots*, the Magician-King, master of the spells that bind. Many of the gods across culture bind unto disease or death. Often binding accompanies the initiation into adulthood or spiritual status. The knots can be used to bind enemies, demons or witchcraft. In the cosmic sphere, the Tao is the chain of creation; the eternal consciousness holds us all in one web of light. In Plato's cave, the humans are bound so that they cannot see behind them, and yet by turning to Ideas man can find his freedom.

My friend Trudy believes that her Twinship bond before and after Judy's death was limiting; it implied responsibilities of keeping the twin engaged and alive. She has decided to become a Single in this part of her life and not obsess over Judy's fate. This decision is wonderful for her.

Are there hard times in Twinship? Throughout the life cycle, it remains difficult to individuate. Separations are both the maturation points and the traumas: different classrooms, different clothes, different friends, not invited to the same parties, leaving for college, boyfriends, marriage, divorce, death of husband, children leaving, moving away, twin death, parents dying. We do not deal well with separation and loss. We grieve. We suffer. We endure terrible loneliness. We find solace with other twins.

The frequency of all twin births in 2015 was 3.4% or 33.5 births out of 1000, an estimated 1 in 30. Identical twins are rare at .45% of all births or 1 in 250 births. Women who are over 30, heavier, taller, with better nutrition, more previous pregnancies and higher estrogen levels are more likely to produce two eggs. Identical twins normally are born in one sac, and fraternal with two sacs. The second-born twin generally has a smaller brain size and weight. Eggs which separate later in the pregnancy provide mirror twins. At nine weeks the twins affect each other in utero, and at 14 weeks they are interacting with each other.

Science has uncovered the phenomena of Epigenetics, the unfolding of genetic tendencies after birth, and clarified the differences in twin fingerprints and development. Nutrition, trauma, disease states and even intentions can cause the genetic material to express differently throughout the life cycle. Longitudinal studies of twins have clarified the contribution of genetics and environment to disease, intelligence, aptitude, and longevity.

Society enjoys a fascination with disappearing or vanishing twins who are absorbed into the other fetus before 12 weeks. In earlier cultures and more recently in The Peoples' Republic of China due to single child restrictions, the second-born twin was often left in the wilderness to die or strangled at birth. The horrors per Stephen King of the evil twin, the amazing similarities of separated twins, and the paranormal powers of twins, such as mental telepathy, have left a strong archetypal imprint in the collective psyche.

Shakespeare in his Comedy of Errors immortalizes the tale of mistaken identity. The horrific and unexpected discovery of a Double by the author Jose Saramago rebounds in literature. Even the facsimile evokes Twinship.

Are the myths true? Twins have a special place in mythology, fairy tales, sacred beliefs of early humanity found in legend, creation and cosmology stories. The twins Romulus and Remus who founded Rome were abandoned in the forest and raised by a She-wolf. Jacob and Esau competed for their birthright and spawned the tribes of Israel. Cain and Abel expressed the homicidal rage of twin competition, with Cain as the incarnation of jealousy and destruction and Abel as the sacrificial victim, the Christ.

Throughout my life, the universe has validated that I am two. Wherever I live, twinness surrounds me. In New York, the Twin Towers, in Colorado the Twin Buttes, the twin rainbows leading to the Colorado house after a spiritual retreat at Canyonlands in Utah. Other twins. The International Association of Twins who contributed dreams for my PhD dissertation 'Do Twins Dream Twin Dreams?' Mothers of Twins. The twin experts, Jane Greer, Nancy Segal, and Barbara Klein, embraced me into their fold.

I received a phone call one day literally out of the blue from a radio station, World Network Radio, asking if I would design a radio show on Twins. The producers offered to shoulder most of the cost if I would contribute somewhat, speaking of an offer that I could not refuse. This program *Twin Talk* broadcasted live for at least two years while I was living with George Lane in Bokeelia, Florida and Durango, Colorado. Another program, *Seeking Serenity*, which also ran for several years, focused on sacred paths up the proverbial mountain. The programs are archived in my website margeryrunyan.com. These interviews are gifts to memorialize Malinda.

They represent a body of knowledge and wisdom that will inform twins throughout the ages, especially because the adult twin experience has not been covered in the clinical literature adequately or truly at all.

The Tao Calls Me

I cannot explain the multiplicity of factors that called me to the Tao. They are a matter of the Heart. Perhaps the Goddesses contacted me from their exalted place in the hierarchy of souls. Perhaps as Carl Jung might say, the answer to the question WHY was yet to come. Just as dreams project the future, a waking dream led me to the greatest source of truth I have since found on this Earth. My encounter with the Taoist system also saved my life.

I only know that somewhere I saw a flyer about a class in the Tao in 1997 and felt a heart attraction. The flyer had a picture of the side view of a human torso with arrows and little fires all around showing the flow of energy. The trainer Ron Diana was teaching the basics of the Tao in his home in Oradell in Northern New Jersey where he returned when he was not teaching in the European capitals with Mantak Chia. Ron was a senior trainer for Mantak and his wife who were among the first Chinese to bring the Tao out of China. He taught us the five-element system, the yin and yang, the Qi, and numerous practices in the times I returned to his home. The Healing Sounds, the Microcosmic Orbit, and Fusion were among the practices we also learned.

My friend Bonnie, still on Earth today at 96, has been my closest companion on this spiritual path. She later traveled to the Catskills to study more deeply. We briefly considered studying at the Healing Tao Center in Thailand, a well-respected destination in the Wellness movement that is still training and healing to this day. Mantak Chia teaches in Europe but not often in the United States.

The Tao is a way of life that is impossible to describe in rational terms. The foundation is energetic and thus defies description except in experience. One can say it is a system of interdependence, the way of nature, the way of everything that flows. The Tao is the nameless origin of all things, ever desireless, the mystery, the doorway to all understanding. The Tao flows everywhere, loves obscurity, and seeks the lowest level like water. There is no controlling center, no cause, no polarity, or effect. The Tao arises mutually with no beginning and no end.

Water symbolizes the flow of the Tao, like a wise old sage with unbound hair walking a mountain path. We are 'in' but not 'of' the earth. We live a human life in order to learn to transcend pain and disease, so it is best to be engaged in human activity while we are here on earth. We are the most whole when our intention is aligned with the Tao and the Divine White Light.

The healing modalities associated with the Tao in Ancient Chinese Medicine are acupuncture, herbs, bodywork, and Medical Qigong. The three areas within the body where energy is stored correspond with the nature of that energy: the lower Dan Tien associates with martial arts and the emotions; the middle Dan Tien associates with medical and the mind; and the upper Dan Tien with the nourishing spirit of the spiritual. These three areas are located at the abdomen, heart, and third eye or forehead.

The Qi is the life force; the Gong is the cultivation; the Tai Chi pole is the vertical channel; the Lower Dan Tien is the power center; the three Wei Ji fields protect us from toxicity in the world such as toxic people, toxic belief systems, toxic bacteria, viruses and other invaders.

The Jing, or essence of the physical body, including blood and lymph, is the innermost field of the body. The Qi or energy is the second field, and the Shen is the outermost boundary of the Self. The physiologic, energetic and spiritual are the Wei Ji fields.

The Yi is thought, belief, intention, mind and consciousness. The Yi influences the Shen or the spiritual energy which in turn influences the Qi. The Qi is the intangible energy that informs the body at the level of emotions. The Qi in turn controls the Jing or the physiological body including the blood, organs, lymph and all that is tangible. If the Yi is out of alignment with divine will or the Tao, the body will manifest a disease state.

After returning to Colorado for two years to study the Three Yana with Lama Tsultrim Allione at Tara Mandala, a Buddhist retreat center, I relocated back to Florida. Then once again, the Tao appeared as an opportunity to learn Medical Qigong in Hallandale, Florida. Fascinated by the curriculum, I contacted Dr. Isaac Goren, a doctor of acupuncture who had studied with Dr. Jerry Allen Johnson. Both were responsible for bringing secret Taoist practices out of China. Dr. Johnson had written five books on Medical Qigong, Chinese Medical Qigong Therapy, which provided extensive information on the history, beliefs and practices of the Chinese Medical Qigong masters, ancient Chinese medicine, which had spawned the practice of acupuncture.

For three years, I attended five-day sessions on five occasions at Dr. Goren's studio, Tao House in Hallandale, Florida, to learn the origin, beliefs, and practices of Medical Qigong. After completing the Practitioner Level, I began using a 20-minutes routine of Medical Qigong. in my psychotherapy practice with astounding results. Clients were leaving the practice room saying they felt so much lighter and freer, that they could feel the Qi circulating through their bodies and had so much more energy.

The awakening of the Practitioner in my experience and training has three levels:

1. The Qigong doctor has increased awareness of her mind and spirit to achieve her true energetic potential which alters forever the way she perceives the world. This includes a heightened sensory awareness, clearer life purpose, and deeper connection to the movement of energy.

2. The practitioner enters the inner sanctuary with greater clarity, an elevated consciousness, deeper self-reflection, and responsibility. She can interrupt karmic flow and has a deeper relationship with the divine.

3. Finally, once she has accessed Wu Ji, the space between heaven and earth, and reprogrammed her mind and core vibration, she becomes her higher self. She has acquired the hidden knowledge of energetic patterns and transcends the time and space continuum.

Divine alignment in the stance of Wu Ji, the empty space between Heaven and Earth, is characterized by these incantations:

1. Divine presence, purify my body in your light.

2. From all levels of my being, purge and release anything that no longer serves my highest purpose.

3. Fill me with love, light, compassion, intelligence, insight, intuition and wisdom that release us from identification with form.

4. Bring me into full alignment with my divine purpose.

The WU JI represents infinite space and provides the field of all potentiality. The Yin is the receptive principle and the Yang the intruding principle. The five Yin organs form constructive and destructive cycles of energy. They also relate to the five Yang organs in the body. A five-element system determines the classification and interrelationships of all experiences. Elements, organs, sounds, tastes, seasons, animals, food, emotions and virtues all fit within the five-element system.

Furthermore, depleting the Qi is slow suicide. A long life in health is the best choice, so we engage in Qigong (the cultivation of the Qi), and we study Medical Qigong or the ancient Chinese medicine for healing others. When we encounter disease, we ask 'how is the person processing her life? Where is the breakdown?' The MQG doctor becomes familiar with the five bodies: spiritual, mental, energetic, emotional and physical, and intervenes on any level to renew the flow. What is blocking the harmonious workings of the entire self? How can we eliminate toxins, which make the whole system work harder and dissipate the Qi?

Habits slow the patterns of energy. We can accept that the future is unpredictable and that the present requires that we be awake. When we can accept this moment as it is, then a portal opens to alert stillness, the transcendent function, an awareness of the deep 'I', the deeper intelligence, insight, intuition and wisdom that release us from identification with form.

When we are practicing Medical QiGong as a doctor treating a patient, there are three levels of healing: healing the disease state, maintaining health into longevity, and feeling the highest potential in alignment with the Tao.

Medical Qigong does not use our Western diagnoses for disease. The doctor is looking for the eight principles in pairs: the yin or yang, hot or cold, wet or dry, excess or deficiency. She is also looking for the organs involved in painful emotions, so that this energy can be transformed to virtue. At the spirit level, she is looking at the effect on the whole system of Maya: delusion, illusion, and thought forms to which we can become attached and thus captured.

We want to be loving, whole, and vibrant, free to discover, express, and manifest our highest life purpose. The purpose of life is finding our way back to the Tao or the light through spiritual evolution. We are programmed to return to God; how long it will take us is our free will. The overly Yang person is grandiose; the overly Yin person is small and weak. We must let go of all these identifications of the ego and surrender to the will of the Tao.

The Fall

Daedalus and Icarus: Daedalus was the architect of the Labyrinth where the Minotaur, half-man half-bull, was imprisoned in Ancient Crete. King Minos, having conquered Athens, required that city state to send twelve youth and maidens as tribute to feed the monster. They were released into the labyrinth and devoured by the monster. In one version, Ariadne unravels a string into the labyrinth and gives it to Theseus, who kills the Minotaur and leads the youth out of the maze. In another version, Daedalus is suspected of betraying the layout to the Athenians, who save their youth. In the latter version, King Minos imprisons Daedalus and his son Icarus on a deserted island for this betrayal. Daedalus designs two pairs of wings from feathers and wax so that the two of them can fly over the water and escape. He warns Icarus not to fly too high in his enthusiasm. Icarus, an exuberant youth, flies too close to the sun. The Sun melts his wax wings and Icarus plunges into the sea to his death. Daedalus survives and takes refuge in Sicily.

One summer night in 1987, while I lay sleeping alone in complete darkness, the phone rang, and my life was changed forever. I had been enjoying a sunny July day swimming and roller skating at my community outside New York City in late July. My parents were spending the month at our summer cottage on Lake Huron in Southampton, Ontario. I had been telling myself, 'I do not mind if I die because on this day, I have known joy.' I was successful in my career with the State of New Jersey, accomplished in my studies with two master's degrees, and still beautiful, slim and healthy at 39. I had a spiritual life with The School of Practical Philosophy in Manhattan that had given me a glimpse of spiritual ascension.

On the other end of the phone was my sister Anne, seven years younger, a college professor and feminist at the University of Cincinnati. Her words froze me. 'I am now going to tell you the hardest thing I will ever have to tell you. Malinda is dead.' My identical twin sister Malinda was dead at 39. She was my life, my love, my joy, my reason for being, my memory, my past, my future, my soul, my higher self. I had not drawn breath without her on earth. My beautiful Malinda with her long brunette hair down to her waist, her beautiful smile, her compassion, her loyalty, her dedication to her students, her fame as a television interviewer, her complete mastery of facts.

She had been declared dead that night after the Royal Canadian Mounties rescued her husband, John and their friends, another couple, from the side of a small mountain outside Montreal, Quebec. They had flown to Quebec in a small plane from their homes in Ithaca, NY, to see the sights in Quebec City and Montreal. The plane had crashed on Mont St. Hilaire near St. Hyacinthe in a rainstorm soon after they took off to return home. Malinda was crushed by the right wing of the plane; she had been sitting in the right back seat when that wing hit a tree on the mountain. The plane dropped and skittered up the hill, eventually coming to a halt. The others were ambulatory, but Malinda's upper body had taken the impact. Her neck was broken; her heart was crushed. They freed her from the plane wreckage and laid her body down. She continued to breathe autonomically with her husband at her side while the other couple climbed down the mountain for help. The helicopters finally found them after circling for many hours. She was so gravely injured that her friends prayed for her to die. At the time of rescue, Malinda was no longer breathing but the authorities took many hours to confirm her death.

Her husband John Efroymson called my sister Anne and her husband Al to give them the horrendous news. My parents vacationing on the shores of Lake Huron at our summer cottage in Southampton, Ontario, were notified by a neighbor, Jack Todd, who had a telephone. My sister Anne was designated to contact me from Cincinnati, Ohio.

In a state of shock, I screamed to the universe and all gods and goddesses, "Bring her back."

I called to her "Come back for me. Where are you? Do not leave me here without you. Take me too," I screamed. I could not breathe.

We had been born together, and we would die together. I lit candles, gathered everything she had ever given me in a pile, begging her to come back.

"Do not ascend, do not leave me, I cannot survive without you." If magic could have pierced the veil of death, she would have been returned. I tried every spell and incantation, every prayer, every plea, and nothing. My own life had ended.

My friend from The School of Practical Philosophy, Sharon, came over from Manhattan the next morning. Her brother had also been killed in a small plane when he was flying stunts at an air show in Oregon. They had watched his plane hit the ground from the stands. Her father was already mentally ill from World War II. She stayed with me until we flew out to Ithaca, NY for the funeral. She slept in the bed with me to keep me alive.

My partner Michael Brinn took a cab from Manhattan that next morning and only returned home to pack. He felt the hugeness of the loss.

Michael and Sharon stayed in Ithaca for the funeral. They stayed very near me because I could not stand the pain. At the funeral, my father cried constantly and from the lectern explained he was wearing his pink pants because he had nothing else at our summer cottage in Ontario. As he spoke, he mesmerized the audience with his hands. My mother read the 23rd Psalm, which had always comforted her. I choked out, 'Malinda was my sun and my moon. She was every part of me.'

Hundreds of people attended, including the students in her learning disability and elementary school classes. The large church was packed. The newspapers covered her death on the front page endlessly. John's mother did not want him to tell the story to us, but we insisted that we hear every detail.

After the funeral people congregated at a large white house on a hill where the hosts served champagne. Videos of Malinda on *More Than the News*, her news show with herself as moderator that she self-produced with her friends, ran in several rooms. I spent weeks after that railing in my own mind against the pilot, whose bad judgment was the cause of the accident per the insurance company for the flying club. I wrote long accusatory letters that I never sent.

Confronting Physical Death

It was July 20, 1987, when she died in the summer of her life, and I had to begin to live without my identical twin at 39 years old. The biggest part of me had also died. My identical twin sister Malinda was gone from our world without a trace, without a goodbye, without warning, without time to prepare. Completely unprepared for a future without her, I saw nothing here on Earth for me. If I could have joined her, I would have gladly done so. I did not know how to suicide nor how to find her in the upper rooms of heaven. Thus began the second half of my life. I never expected in that moment to live to the age of 72 and beyond. I have lived a long life since her death, 34 years without her and yet not a day without her. Once a twin, always a twin.

Sudden death evokes the film *The Unbearable Lightness of Being*, which I watched in a theater with Michael Brinn soon after Malinda was killed. Eastern Europeans from Poland who survived Soviet oppression and much danger during the revolution ultimately succumbed to a car crash at the height of their freedom in the United States. I screamed in pain at the injustice of it. Michael could not console me.

In 2019, a yoga student at our studio in Florida mounted her three-wheeled red bike with her helmet affixed securely. I bid her farewell. She only made it thirty yards up the road to be killed by a speeding driver. I was the last person to see her alive.

Is there a moment when we reach a Pinnacle of Joy, when we surrender fully to a higher purpose beyond this Earth? Do we accept this Fate?

Malinda's friend Jack wrote a poem to memorialize her in the week after her death. He was inconsolable as we all were.

> A hundred times, these
> few days, I have wept as so
> many others,
> recalling your smile, the
> sweetness of your soul, the
> gentleness,
> in countless
> kindnesses, you
> bestowed on
> everyone.
> No solace now, except in
> dreams, where I have seen your
> nurturing soul by the healing
> waters,
> too far from my waking
> heart, too distant from
> daylight's calling.
>
> But last night, in a dream,
> I saw you as a girl, the
> cares of years on this
> difficult earth, like
> ripples of pebbles
> thrown into peaceful waters,
> dissolving into smoothness once
> again. And I awoke with greeting,
> not farewell, weeping with the
> pleasure of my vision,
> my sorrow for a moment
> staunched. your dreams of life
> ebbing only
> from these waking shores.

Jack Williams

Icarus was joyful and carefree. He could not contain his love of flying. My twin sister Malinda felt this way. She loved to soar through the skies on the little planes that she and her friends rented. She believed in the joy of flying. She did not express fear. She expected that her life would be successful and long, that she had escaped from whatever prisons had held her and that she was ready to soar, that these friends could be trusted, that the weather was good enough to fly, that she could fly close to the sun. In literal terms, Icarus' fate befell her.

The next year I boarded a helicopter to see the lava running to the sea in Hawaii. I was sitting in the right rear seat. It was then that I felt her fear. I developed a fear of heights that plagued me on carnival rides, terraces, airplanes, cliff sides, thin pathways and tall buildings. A phobia. A fear of falling.

The questions that occupied my mind for hours each day:

> Did I have forewarning?
> What could I have done differently to cheat the Fates?
> Did I feel her fear and aloneness on that mountain?
> Did she accept physical death?
> Can I still feel her?
> Is an aspect of her still here? Where is she?
> Is there a path? Where does it begin?
> Did the wrong twin die? Is there a grand plan?
> Where is the rest of me?
> How will I find myself and my lost soul pieces? Will the pain lessen?
> How will I recover from her loss?
> Will I have to start my life over again? Am I still a twin?
> Will I ever fit into the world again? Can I live for two?
> How will I survive?
> Do I want to survive here on earth? How long do I have to stay here?
> What do I truly believe? Will I love that way again?
> How can I keep her memory alive? Will I ever become whole?
> Who will help me? Will I see her again?

The Twin World enveloped me like a shroud and slowly I became willing to accept my destiny as a twinless twin. There was No Exit from this Hell, as the Jean Paul Sartre play illuminates. Malinda and I had chosen to incarnate on Earth as twins, separated in the womb, yet forever joined. The paradox of integration and individualization became my psychic life.

A Watery Burial

That following summer the remaining family met at the cottage on Lake Huron in Southampton. Michael and Shahrazad, my little Shih Tzu, traveled with me. I remember Michael in the bedroom where my grandmother, Margaret Parker Sisson whom we called Mernie, used to sleep at the top of the stairs to the right. When the day came to disburse Malinda's ashes in Lake Huron behind Chantry Island, Michael declined to participate. He asked to be excused due to the feelings of grief and despair that my family was experiencing. He decided to end the relationship soon thereafter. I did not understand at that time that I would need to descend into hell and take that journey alone.

We rode out as a family onto Lake Huron in the motorboat that my brother-in-law Albert Kanters kept at the dock on the Saugeen River where my father loved to fish in his little rowboat. Al motored us out off the coast of Southampton to a place in the deep, clear water above the huge volcanic rocks. It was behind the ever-present Chantry Island, where the seagulls and cormorants lived by the old, abandoned lighthouse. When we put Malinda's ashes into Lake Huron as a stream of white descending into the darkness of the deep, a white seagull flew over the boat. My father asked my mother if she believes in transmigration. She said yes. From that moment, Malinda was a seagull. We heard *Let It Be* by the Beatles playing, even though we were far from the shore and beyond the reach of the cottages. Later I had an insight that I too would be dissolved into Lake Huron as in alchemy, and that I would return to the water of the womb where we were first joined.

How does a single twin find the courage and meaning to stay in life alone? I had no faith, no hope, no plan, no love of life. With Malinda's death, I was embarking on a spiritual journey that would lead me to the depths of my own soul. The ancient sciences would provide the blueprint for that heroine's journey, including the Joseph Campbell monomyth of the path through the dark woods to find the holy grail, the fountain of youth, the universal truth, and the return to Community to serve the Other. The helpers on that journey were found inside myself as I explored my inner life and studied psychoanalysis, analytic psychology, astrology, mythology, tarot, Gnosticism, the afterlife, alchemy, philosophy, existentialism, phenomenology, Theosophy, Taoism, Buddhism, Hinduism and spirituality. I was determined to understand the Unconscious and the Supra-conscious and to generate a belief system that would lead me to Malinda.

If I had continued to believe in the Christian Heaven and Hell, I surely would have suicided in order to join Malinda in Heaven if I could have achieved that holy place with a lifetime of Sin.

The words of twins.

I do not think I could physically live without my sister.
We do everything together all the time.
We spend every waking moment with each other.
We feel like we are in a hall of mirrors. We are
soul mates in two-part harmony.
You are never alone.
I consider us being ONE. She is my other half.
We love to look the same, to be the same.
We are married to each other, 'til death do us part.'
Independence was not worth the sacrifice.
We have the intimacy that most long for.
Nothing can separate us. The acceptance is irresistible.
We revel in attention.
Everyone should have a twin. It is the best thing in the world.

The Suffering

Malinda was 'the wind beneath my wings.' She was 'the Rose' who emerged from the winter into a spring of blossoming. These songs from Bette Midler were my inner thoughts; I sang and sang to console myself.

Two nights after Malinda's death an angel named Dr. Raymond Brandt called me. I was standing in the kitchen of the Harmon Cove condominium on Harbor Key in Secaucus. I still have frequent dreams about that community where I lived for 26 years in sight of the Trade Towers. He told me about his brother's death; they were both working on electrical lines for the power company and his brother was electrocuted. We cried and cried together. He had founded Twinless Twins but had not yet incorporated it. I wrote him a long letter explaining my impressions that I was not 'less,' that Malinda was still inside me, and that I would become 'more.' He did not agree and in fact he did not understand.

Dr. Brandt became a frequent phone contact. One day he asked me for a donation to the fledgling organization Twinless Twins. I suggested that he incorporate the organization as a non-profit to protect himself around the donations of money. We discussed the name of the group again. I felt like I was More of a twin than ever and wanted to celebrate my continuing Twinship. All the twins in the Twin World were my twins and I had the capacity to Twin with other people in my life. In fact, I had already been married at 24 to Bob Gorman, a fraternal twin to Bonnie, from Watertown, Massachusetts. There was no solid explanation for marrying a twin, but I had come to understand that twins live in a different world from singles. I wanted to be a Forever Twin or a Twin More Twin, not Less of something. I already knew that I had a long road to go to introject her into myself, and I wanted this hard work acknowledged. Dr. Brandt was adamant even though I was very angry at him, an inevitable component of the grief process. Later he became an icon and saint to the Twinless Twins, still active, and he wrote a piercing book about Twin Loss.

The Twinless Twins organization is still filled with members who believe they are less because of their loss. The focus remains on grieving and grieving and grieving. Mary Morgan, a daughter of Nelson Rockefeller, has a strong hold on the organization. She runs a large group at every annual conference in which she helps the twins process their grief. The board members do not want any discussion of dreams, afterlife communication, Carl Jung, or eastern spiritual beliefs. For the most part they are completely identified with their grief. The meetings focus on reliving the death over and over.

Every attendee tells the story of his or her loss. Then we cry and cry. My friend Linda Pountney invited me to do a group on after life connection, which 50 or 60 people attended. Everyone in the group had had afterlife communication through animals, birds, and dreams. This conference was the only one I ever attended. The board decided that I was too far out there! My esoterism went beyond their capacity to incorporate.

Dr. Jane Greer treated me in individual psychotherapy after Malinda's death. A synchronicity brought me to her: I had been reading an article in the Local Section of the New York Times in 1987 about a twin organization that was meeting at a restaurant in New York City. I discussed attending with Malinda, and we also planned to attend Twinsville in Ohio, a gathering of 3000 twin sets in August. Malinda died in the interim. As Michael and I had planned to go in advance, we carried through. There I met the twins who would save my life one more time. Two twins, young men adopted at birth by a loving family, were chairing the group at this moment. They invited me to their home and consoled me with loving twin surround. Then these lovely young men referred me to Dr. Jane Greer, the consultant for the twin loss arm of the organization that eventually became Twinless Twins. Dr. Greer was practicing in Manhattan and Bergenfield, NJ as a Licensed Clinical Social Worker in partnership with a psychiatrist who could prescribe medications to her clients.

My life had become an endless trek from Secaucus to the hospital in Newark. There my blood was drawn to determine if I could inject Coumadin, for fertility, that evening. I would circle back to meet with Dr. Greer, stopping at a payphone in a diner to get my marching orders. I had been trying to get pregnant with Michael Brinn. He had a loft in Tribeca with a huge window looking Uptown, and I owned my condominium in Secaucus between the Holland and Lincoln Tunnels on the Hackensack River. He arranged that we would meet on weekends. I was very lonely during the week, and he preferred living alone. Ultimately, I had joined a Single Women's group composed of women wanting children in Manhattan and started the endless and discouraging infertility treatments. I was taking Prozac and grieving my whole life to that point in time. I truly did not want to live. I was drinking heavily.

The archetype of the right wing began to pervade my consciousness.

Malinda had been crushed by the right wing of the plane. I had packed angel earrings made of glass and the right side broke in transit. I decorated the house in Durango with glass angels and the right wing fell and shattered. I remembered that I played right wing in field hockey before our society fell in love with soccer. My right hand is dominant, and I developed a terrible constriction in my right shoulder, which forced me into chiropractic and massage. My masseuse stated that we grieve women on the right side. My neck was badly dislocated just as Malinda's had been during the accident.

My heart was so heavy as her heart had been crushed.

I disclosed the after-life communication to Dr. Greer, who ultimately wrote the book *After-Life Connection*. I was Alexa, who revealed the twin powers to her after my sister died. Dr. Isaac Goren, my Taoist master, practiced Shen Gong while I rested on the table, and I revealed the weakness of my right shoulder. I had thoughts such as 'I am not whole. I am weak. I have a wound that will not heal.' After his treatment, the arm improved dramatically. I often sing the Blackbird Fly song, 'Fix that broken wing and learn to fly...' At the cottage, we rescued a seagull with a broken right wing and put it in a cardboard box in the old barn (now a fancy cottage). I do not remember its fate.

This was a true descent into the darkest regions I have ever explored. I could not stop crying unless I went to my office in Newark, where I worked for the NJ Department of Human Service. I lay on my bed for hours trying to figure out where Malinda had gone. If she had gone to heaven, how could I be sure to get there with her? Would suicide work? How could we be together? I had never felt so alone and so far from humanity. I was one half of a whole. I had lost all my power, all my uniqueness, all my plans and dreams in one moment. How could a universe that was so cruel hope to keep me here? This earth was a veil of tears, and I had absolutely no idea how I was going to continue to live in such a horrible place. The future was unimaginable. The length of each day was interminable.

The Descent

During the descent into Hell where I must confront my own death, I fell into deep depression, shame, guilt, and despair that would I ever see her again? I would prefer to die than take this journey without her, but I did not understand my choices.

HEKATE (Hecate) was the goddess of magic, witchcraft, the night, moon, ghosts and necromancy. She was the only child of the Titans, Perses and Asteria, from whom she received her power over heaven, earth, and sea. Persephone had been kidnapped by Pluto, the god of Hades, and forced to become his wife. Her mother Demeter, the goddess of agriculture and the seasons, made endless winter until Pluto relented and allowed Persephone to visit her mother during spring and fall. Hecate assisted Demeter in her search for Persephone after she had been kidnapped, guiding Demeter through the night with flaming torches. After the mother-daughter reunion, Hekate became Persephone's minister and companion in Hades. Hekate's companions are the Furies, winged creatures who punish wrongdoers. She governs the crossroads and stands fiercely at the joining of the three roads.

She is my identity as a goddess.

Aeneas, the Trojan prince in Virgil's Aeneid, accompanies Sybil the wise old woman into the underworld to see his father Anchises and find out his journey. He learns that many can enter Hades, but very few ever leave. Sybil requires that he bring a golden bough to pacify Pluto the god of Hades.

Charon ferries him across the River Acheron (Styx), and they pass the guard Cerberus, the three-headed monster. Turning right they find the Elysian Field where souls await a thousand years to be reincarnated again. Anchises his father predicts Aeneas' future, the founding of Rome. Perhaps I had the golden bough, or I would never have left this Hell.

"Trojan, Anchise's son, the descent of Avernus is easy.
All night long, all day, the doors of dark Hades stand open.
But to retrace the path, to come up to the sweet air of heaven, That is labor indeed." (Virgil, The Aeneid)

As Peter, Paul and Mary sang about Puff the Magic Dragon, 'Without his lifelong friend Puff could not be brave, so Puff that Mighty Dragon sadly slipped into his cave,' I went into the cave of the deepest darkness and depression that anyone could have ever known. I lay on my bed in an abyss of pain and prayed to die. My friend and fellow twin, Dr. Nancy Segal, was researching twin loss at this exact time. I completed my survey of my feelings and later she reached significant conclusions that twin loss is more painful than any other loss on earth.

During this period of survival in an abyss of pain, I became invisible to the outside world. Without an identity as a Twin, I no longer belonged in my body nor on this Earth. I was no longer powerful. I was no longer special. I was no longer alive. I became Hecate, Kali, Sybil, the goddesses of darkness.

For months after that I could not stop crying. All I remember is praying to join her in heaven and not knowing how. I only stopped crying when I was committed to functioning in my career as a contract administrator for the State of New Jersey. My friend, a huge black man who had retired from military intelligence, Art Lovett, would let me sit in his lap and cling to him until I could stop sobbing. I regressed into childhood.

I would go home from work, put on my cassettes of Sweet Honey in the Rock, and listen to 'In the Upper Room with Jesus.' Sobbing. I listened for hours to the Broadway song track of *Les Misérables* and in particular the song about 'empty chairs and empty tables, where my friends will drink no more.' Another song comforted me, 'She flew so high she touched the sky.' I knew that Malinda was a bird, perhaps a seagull, a mourning dove. Mourning doves have followed me everywhere since her death. Even here at my home in Florida 40 years later, they perch on the phone wire. I often remember Joni Mitchell's song, "Bird on a Wire."

My descent into despair was a veil of tears fueled with endless crying. I felt myself being pulled into a deep, dark hole. I could not get a handle on myself. Emptiness. My thoughts were 'I can no longer live in a world where Malinda is not. I cannot endure a world so cruel as to take her from me. I no longer belong here, but where do I belong? Where is she? Can I get to her?' I thought about suicide constantly. All I remember is praying to join her in heaven and not knowing how. If I could have joined her through an act of will, I would have been gone. I hesitated to commit suicide because I feared I would go to a place where I could not find her. Perhaps I would go to a hell for souls who suicide and not to the place where good people like Malinda were privileged to reside for eternity.

I could feel my partner Michael pulling away from me, and I did not care. Michael Brinn was a handsome and brilliant man who lived in Tribeca in NYC and worked as a stock proxy solicitor. We had been dating for eight years. One of our favorite haunts was his parents' home in the Catskills, Swan Lake near Monticello. He was not interested in marriage and had made it clear that he would not stay with any woman long. One day he called me at my home across the Lincoln Tunnel in New Jersey to end our relationship. I asked if this was what eight years had come to and he answered, 'apparently.' I was not the fun-loving woman whom he once adored. This past year, I located him in Cape Coral near my home in Bokeelia, FL, and we shared our experiences of those 30 years. He had changed his lifestyle after we separated. I received no amends. For many nights I dreamed about him. I was still fascinated by him and adored him.

Carl Jung, in his book, The*Red Book,* perfectly describes where we go when faced with the acute traumas of life. I dove deep into my own unconscious world, recognizing that peace would not be found on the horizontal plane of the collective consciousness. The frequency where I was resonating was too low for my heart to hear any longer. I lost interest in friendships, socialization of any kind, going out to dinner and movies, traveling, awards and honors. The Tao had captured my attention, and I delved more deeply into the world of energy healing. I went to Tibetan Buddhist retreats such as the *Three Yanas* at Tara Mandala with Lama Tsultrim Allione. Meditations collected in my psyche.

The inner world became my best friend. Reading Jung, specifically *The Red Book*, finally published in May of 2000, confirmed that I was taking the right path. Jung resigns from his outer responsibilities and roles in the world of psychoanalysis and goes into his dream life where he finds the primary archetypes informing his soul during this lifetime. Astrology and tarot fascinated me. I went deeper and deeper into my Self, seeking the symbols that would lead me into an archetypal world. There I was seeking the meaning of all this loss and suffering on Earth and the power to ascend spiritually into Malinda's world.

By then, the archetype of the labyrinth had captured my imagination. The cathedral at Chartres became my active dream, as I circumambulated the inner world of mySelf and my eternal Soul. My friend Dorothy and I were privileged to spend two days at Chartres in October of 2018. There we gazed into the radiance of the stained-glass windows and enjoyed charcuterie while the wondrous luminaires filled our hearts with Joy.

The labyrinth is a journey from the outside visible world to the inside invisible world of the unconscious and the supra-conscious. In archetypal terms, this walk is a return to the womb, a descent into the underworld, a journey to the center of the world. These rites of initiation into the esoteric require that the Minotaur be slain in the heroic struggle with animal passion. The initiate as the heroine Ariadne returns via the umbilical thread that ties us to the source of life.

This descent disturbs rational consciousness while the initiate loses her way, thus opening to the transcendent function. The fear is unbearable, and courage is the tipping point. Courage is not the absence of fear but the strength to walk through it.

Pema Chodron, the Buddhist nun, weaves the tale of the monks walking in the forest when a tiger jumps out. The monks scatter except for one who confronts the tiger, the incarnation of fear. The fear dissipates and flees from the steady gaze of the courageous. The initiate perseveres through the trials and emerges into the light. The transcendent function allows the initiate to merge the seeming paradox of separation and wholeness, which the twin world incarnates, into a new level of consciousness, a wholeness with the Self. Shining light through locked doors and down dark hallways, the heroine shares a oneness with all creation.

When we find ourselves in the midst of such earthly pain, the responsible self must face the shadow. I attribute this truth to Murray Stein, a current Jungian with whom I have shared many ideas. We must turn inward in order to digest our own evil and the collective evil. The new wholeness allows this process to happen.

I became fascinated with the afterlife. A Jungian expert in Vermont contacted me and provided an individualized class on the theories of the afterlife. We read excerpts from the Tibetan Book of the Dead about Bardo and the bright lights that indicate choices of reincarnation or Buddhahood. I practiced meditation and compassion, believing that I could attain full enlightenment and join Malinda as a Buddha. She asked us to answer the question: When you die, what do you expect will happen to you?

I wrote: 'My spirit will travel through a dark tunnel and then into light... I will recognize other spirits. We will have deep peace and know Oneness and Knowingness. There will be music, resonance and vibration. We are a group of souls meeting over and over. The masters will review our karmic status. I will have the chance to reincarnate.'

Clarissa Pinkola Estes in *Women Who Run with the Wolves* analyzes a fairy tale about the girl who loses her hands, *La Selva Subterranea: the Underground Initiation*. I rediscovered this classic and reminded myself that the Handless Maiden lost her hands, her agency, to the Devil. She wanders through the state of unconsciousness in the land of the dead. She has the endurance of the lone wolf and can bear the exile of the initiate. The descent will nourish her in the dark even when she has lost her way. Like Persephone and all the Death/Life/Death goddesses, she has enough spiritual consciousness to know that she will find the Tree of Life and meet the old crone who has much to teach women. She also cries and cries and knows that she is conscious; one cannot go back to sleep when one is crying.

Identical twins do not individuate without a struggle. I understood fully that I was on a spiritual journey. The Victim of Circumstance without power or agency must find the courage to transcend into the Manifestation stage when we realize that the universe is manifested By us and For us as co-creators. Then the Servant stage arrives when we use our good will and power to love and serve others through the agency of our own hands. We accept that the universe exists Through us. Finally, we become Whole knowing that the Universe exists As us, as the Oneness of all creation.

Johannes Brahms: A German Requiem, 1868

'Blessed are they that mourn, for they shall have comfort.
They that sow in tears shall reap in joy.
Who goeth forth and weepeth, and beareth precious seed,
Shall doubtless return with rejoicing and bring his sheaves with him.'

The Trials

At the age of 23 in 1974, I was working as a caseworker for the Division of Youth and Family Services in New Jersey on the mean streets of Jersey City, Hoboken, Bayonne and the rest of Hudson County directly across the Hudson River from Manhattan. My husband Bob and I had moved from Cape Cod, his original haunts, to a condominium community, Harmon Cove, so that he could be town attorney for Secaucus, NJ. Malinda had relocated with her new partner John to Washington, DC where they were teaching elementary school. We had bonded with worthy men and felt safe with each other.

One morning in the ghetto of Jersey City, I was descending the stairs from visiting a family when two men grabbed me and dragged me into the basement of the tenement. Their intention was robbery, which I foiled by swallowing my engagement and wedding rings. One of the men stayed behind and raped me on a pile of garbage in the foyer. I remained motionless until I felt assured they had left the neighborhood, then jumped into the State car I had been driving and circled the streets, stopping people to ask the location of the police station. My supervisor met me at the police station, and we proceeded to the hospital. Bob joined me at the Jersey City Medical Center where a rape kit was administered. I screamed, 'Do not leave me alone in this room.' Bob and Mary accompanied me home where Bob offered me a glass of whiskey. The feeling of relaxation remained in my psyche and became my default position.

Then the axe fell. Panic. Panic. Claustrophobia. Agoraphobia. Men staring at me. Black men staring at me. No elevators. No stairwells. No dark streets. No streets at all.

Anorexia. Counting bites. Counting meals. Staring at my stomach to see if it had swollen. No sex. No touching me. Screaming and crying. Drinking.

I started an affair with a fellow caseworker at the Jersey City office, later my second husband, Hank Walker. Hank was big and strong, grew up in Jersey City, and knew the mean streets. He would wait for me after work to ensure that the State car was safely parked in the enclosed lot and that I had caught the bus to Secaucus. Gradually, my marriage failed until Bob fell in love with one of our friends and I released him. I was 30 with a severe case of PTSD, divorced, isolated, alcoholic, flooded with anxiety. Hank eventually left for Denver to work for United Airlines. I had not one single friend. My family was clustered in Ohio, and I kept all my secrets to myself.

I had several other close calls in the ghetto. Once when I was taken hostage while men with guns circled the apartment. Another day in Newark, alone at my car in a secluded parking lot, two men grabbed me, put a knife to my throat and stole my purse. They surely could have abducted me. My dear friend Art Lovett, another student at the Rutgers University School of Social

Work, promoted me out of casework into a program development position with the Division of Youth and Family Services, which launched my career.

Art was a huge black man who had worked in Army intelligence. After his wife died of cancer, I thought we would get together, but he chose his family instead -his mother and two children. A younger white woman would not have blended. I realize that I am searching for big men who can protect me.

Charlotte Klein MD., a psychiatrist who practiced at Bellevue, a notorious psychiatric hospital in Manhattan, treated me weekly at her home in Bergen County, NJ. For the first time in my early 30's, I confronted my co-morbidities in all their glory. She used her hands to illustrate the serotonin reuptake with her palm as the nucleus of the neuron. Her fingers represented the ganglia and dendrites while the synapse was the space between the two hands. How many times have I repeated this metaphor for clients who desperately desire to understand neurotransmitters and the effect of addiction and mental illness on the chemistry of the brain? To accept oneself as a complex organism rather than a set of hopeless thoughts and self-criticism brings remarkable relief. At one point, as I am in my car on the Turnpike Extension leading away from the George Washington Bridge, I come face to face with the reality of my clinical depression, alcoholism and PTSD. Why me? I am a gifted young woman who works hard. What have I done to deserve this?

Of course, I had already decided that my mother could not judge me fairly. She screamed so horribly and hated me so completely that I decided I would just accept the bad twin label and buy my freedom from her. I became the free spirit who flew away from her system of martyrdom, her blaming and the guilt. That worked for me. The family coalesced to exclude me and to make me into the identified patient. I colluded by cutting them off in my 50s for six or seven years, so that I would not be Poor Margery any longer. That is when I named myself Mercy during my study of Buddhism at Tara Mandala in Pagosa Springs.

Women who are raped are 26 times more likely to develop addiction than the general public. Alcoholism is a progressive and fatal disease. I drank and drank to deal with the anxiety, the shame, the loneliness, the terror of my own suicidal thoughts. At 58 years of age, after my family had labeled and abandoned me, I joined AA and achieved sobriety. I attended at least one meeting per day for 90 days (90 and 90) and reached one year through progressive months of support from AA. My sponsor, Karen S., was gentle and accepting. She worked the 12 Steps with me. My monthly coins were my greatest joy. Then months turned into years, and alcoholism no longer plagued me. I am still cautious about being around alcohol and people who are using it. I have fifteen years of sobriety since that fortuitous decision to put down the drink. My sobriety date is July 8, 2006.

My beloved sponsor, Karen S, taught me the best 10th step I have ever heard. At the end of each day, ask four questions:

1. What did I do to love and respect myself today?

2. What did I do to love someone else today?

3. Where did I see love/light/miracles today?

4. What could I have done better?

5. Pray for grace and the insight to see the bigger picture.

When my mother visited me in Florida after I had begun my walk on the path of sobriety, I raged at her for hours. George had taken me into his home and dedicated himself to my sobriety. Hank was in jail in Lee County after he was arrested several times for drunk driving. He had also been charged with drunk driving in Albuquerque, New Mexico. My mother and I went to see him at the Ortiz Lee County Jail. We stood outside a chain link fence, and he appeared behind bars, lurching, pale, confused, and malnourished. He fell to the floor of the cell at one point. We spoke to the jail authorities to determine his diet and health condition. Naturally, they denied any maltreatment. After that visit, I screamed and screamed at my mother. She had not protected me. She had not advised me. She had not nurtured me. The wrong twin died. Malinda was compliant, and I in contrast had escaped from my mother's net of martyrdom, gifting to buy love, dissimulating, blaming, projecting her shadow onto me and my father.

I credit my partner, George Lane, now deceased for walking the walk with me. He had 28 years of sobriety when he relapsed before his impending death at 79. He died in the bed with our Weimaraner Sasha, now 15, and me on March 31, 2012. We buried him in Rochester, New York with full honor guard for his military service at the Tomb of the Unknown Soldier at Arlington Cemetery. His police compatriots in Rochester also provided full honors.

How can I ever explain the pain of rape and subsequent alcoholism? By the time Malinda was killed, I was already weakened by these dual traumas. I hated myself. I lived in shame, secrecy and guilt. My shadow haunted me mercilessly. No wonder I believed that the wrong twin died. These dreams that I have chosen to share represent my constant fears of attack, my ostracism from normal society, my continuous alcoholic dreams after sobriety, my self-destruction and hopelessness. I WAS SPLIT.

In my journal I wrote, 'I am ashamed of my mental illness. I have PTSD. I get enraged and scream. I threaten. I hate people who are incompetent and cannot listen.

I am afraid of my emotional weakness, my depths, my rage, my own insanity. Sad, mad, glad, afraid, quite simple. I am selfish. I am seeking my own self in the eyes of other people. Three prayers: thank you, help, use me. I am looking after children, perhaps the child in myself. I am lost and tired. I am homeless. I am seeking the sacred and it eludes me.'

Nightmares

Looking through my dream references, I find Ernest Hartmann MD Dreams and Nightmares, the pages of which I had highlighted while writing my dissertation. His Freudian bent is comforting. Dreams after trauma have emotional processing at their heart: at first, terror, fear, vulnerability, and later survival and survivor guilt. The dream contextualizes the emotion through condensation, which collapses people, places, and events into compound images and metaphors. The trauma is gradually integrated into the psyche. He advises that the most striking image is the place to start the dream interpretation. Dreamers with more characters in their dreams such as twins, which my dissertation found significant, have thinner boundaries and integrate more quickly; they are empathetic and creative, oversensitive and vulnerable. Dreams are so effective in emotional integration because they avoid over-learned patterns in consciousness and thus make broader connections. Later, this understanding became familiar but at the time I had no opening through which to glimpse the healing at work.

07/27/07 I snuck into a SunTrust conference. The powerful men came into the front. I went right up there and talked to one of them. My skirt was too short. My hair was wrong. I feared discovery. I wanted a job. Then a woman who had been nice came to me in the power area and said, 'Get out; you don't even work here.' Then I went to another conference next door, a shipping company, also disguising myself as an employee, also mostly women except the powerful men. I finally asked one of the women if she thought I would ever get a job there and she said, 'No. The young women start here and learn very technical skills, then advance in the company.' I was disappointed and felt left out of everything.

Comment: I am now a twinless twin and do not fit in either world.

04/10/08 I am screaming and crying in rage. I knew I was insane. George had invited many men over to drink at the bar without telling me. I was threatening to kill them. They were looking at me like I was crazy. I knew somehow that I was alienating everyone but could not stop raging.

7/29/08 A woman who worked with me in Bergen County, NJ took me on a wild ride through Newark's black ghetto neighborhoods trying to rob me and dump me. She kept acting like she was helping me and was simply lost driving me home. Then I noticed that my fanny pack was gone. Finally, I was terrified walking in Newark alone and found my way to my former workplace on Raymond Blvd. It was dangerous in that neighborhood. Then the police said that the two women were a ring who stole from people and dumped them. All of a sudden, the whole journey made sense. I went to

Bergen County to tell them. She was going to be replaced. I investigated a big room with two men working and then closed the door. Then I went back to Raymond Blvd. in Newark, NJ, to my office. I had not been there for a while. There were clothes in several closets. I tried to collect and consolidate. I decided to tell the truth to my colleague. We got down to whisper. He said, 'You could have walked away, gotten a cab.' I could not justify my feelings of terror and imprisonment. My grandmother was the main receptionist who sat at the front desk. I wanted to tell her, but she was in the bathroom not feeling well.

Comment: I cannot tell anyone the truth. No one is listening.

08/08 I was in a class about Star Wars with a famous star lecturing from a lectern. The phone rang and it was for Malinda. She was listening, so I snuck away to get the call. A woman said, 'I am worried about another person; she has not come to work.' I followed the man into an apartment. A sad, pregnant woman entered the apartment to meet him. We were all speaking French. I was practicing and, in the dream, remembered French. The man was distant. He had brought some presents for her - a beautiful tea set and some fancy food. I cared for her, helped her unwrap the present, then propped her back up. The man left and then I left with her and walked her out. I was still looking for the disappeared woman. I went back to the last class. A big fat man/baby gave me the class location from a desk at the front. Another class had spilled out onto the street. He said that was the tattoo class. I thought 'What am I supposed to be learning at this place?' He directed me into a nearby apartment to look for the missing woman. There was a baby with wise eyes on the bed. He grew and said, 'Teach me about sex.' He talked with his mind. I thought, 'Am I the man or the woman?' Then I looked at his little penis under his robe and laughed- no way. He was too small. I noticed a handsome man coming towards the apartment. He was going to enter by the front door. I was scared and trapped. I noticed a back door with a screen. I stepped into the little storm area, waited until he made noise at the front door and then opened the trap door, and walked away quickly.

Comment: The disappearing woman is Myself. The baby is Myself sexualized after rape. The apartment reminds me of many apartment buildings where I went to see clients and then panicked when I heard people behind me on the stairs. I was terrified of dead ends such as the stairway where I had been raped.

7/7/09 Bob (my first husband) and Karen (his second wife), Anne and Al were going to a big house in Colorado. Karen was jealous. Where was I going to sleep? Donuts for breakfast. Got coffee. The waitress wanted too much money at the window. I walked away. I rollerbladed back through the wet and snowy town. Got my clothes from a thrift shop; they are mine. A large waterfall then a path to the right of it. How was I going to make it? Snowy, cold. I wanted to call Bob for help.

Comment: Bob lived with me during the rape and afterwards until he could bear it no longer. He was hugely helpful during this period.

7/7/11 George, a composite older woman and a man both old and young, driving us in a big truck. I was one of the drivers with a key and curly hair. Every time we climbed up a straight ladder on the back to get into the drivers' seat. I was sometimes afraid that I would fall or slip. Once near home Exit 15 or 16 of the NY Turnpike we stopped at a mobile home that they owned, and we ate a special meal. Thanksgiving. The food was plentiful and informal.

No dining room table, just temporary plates from which we grabbed some food. George was full-bodied, full throated, laughing, anxious to get home. When we went outside it was a black ghetto and I asked why are these people helping us?

Comment: With George I am always safe. He was an ex-police sergeant.

1/05/12 In a neighborhood gambling and drinking. Hank was loose and out of control, drinking, planning to join a gambling game and I knew it was all trouble.

1/15/12 In Harmon Cove druggies were living down the hall. It was my ex-partner's room, and he must have told them where to sleep. Hank and I were getting ready to go away for the weekend. I had washed my hair, brushing it out. The druggies came back with a gun. The manager would not evict them or charge them with trespassing. Then they came back and the leader had a gun. I asked him for it on the stairs. He let it hang. The adults left - said they were not welcome there. Someone had left pictures at the front desk. I was wiping the pictures of current events when the top veneer came off and underneath were old photos of my childhood with Malinda. I was pleased with the old photos - in color. Then the druggies turned into homeless children. We were trying to catch them. They were lawless and wily. I held one down with my foot - tried to tie another one but the string broke. They were all still free. A gal from the hotel was calling for help. My right hand would not move, I woke up lying on it.

06/04/12 In Albuquerque with Sharon, a friend from the School of Practical Philosophy, and Bob, my ex-husband. We are looking at a condo, just a shell for the homeless with a canal nearby. We were headed to Durango and stopped here. A man had just found out that his wife was cheating. I needed to take him home. I took our wheeled vehicle and let him off in an elevator shaft. He was angry and crazy. When I got back Bob was gone to the hospital with asthma. I thought, 'How are we going to get to Durango? It is extremely high altitude there.' The man came back with his wife. We were near a pool. The woman got on a bus and got off, and I drove back to Jewish Family Services. A woman was with me. A man said, 'She gets rides all the time.' She hid under a box on a chute. She got caught and the director brought a disabled woman to say, 'This is what happens.' The woman did not care. I climbed out of the truck area, then hitched a ride on the back of a departing truck. I kept thinking, "What am I doing here?" I need to get to Durango. How will I find Bob, and will he be able to go? I am lost in a strange city and do not even know where I am. Just keep going. You will figure it out.'

Comment: Am I also the disabled woman warning myself not to get out of bounds?

6/15/13 I was riding my bike for an interview as a rape crisis counselor in Bonita Springs, FL. I was soaring along south thru rural Bergen County, lots of small towns, like another dream, back roads, dirt roads until I realized I definitely was late. I stopped at a hair salon and could not see the number or dial it. I kept looking at different pieces of paper with the writing too small. My phones were disappearing, and the numeric pad was changing and incomprehensible. I was crying and distraught asking people to help me.

They were apprehensive and some moved away. One woman thought I was calling the agency for help. Time was passing: 6 pm, then 6:15 pm and I could not get through to them on the phone. I was afraid they would consider me not interested and yet I was perfect for the job.

Comment: People are repelled by my emotional behavior.

8/17/14 There was a party of family and old friends - only one bottle of vodka, so a few of us went looking for a liquor store. A composite friend Sharon or Julie Drew. In one place we had to walk through a marketplace until we got to a crowded window. The store charged six hundred dollars and we used Julie's check to get one vodka and one wine. I was shocked at how much they charged and so we returned them. Then we found another window and they said that they could sell us one bottle each and so we bought them. By then it was hours later, and I wondered if people at the party were annoyed that we had no alcohol.

Comment: Drunk dreams were common with me after sobriety.

8/30/15 I was enrolling in classes. Long line. Missing classes and wondering how to get the notes. I did not have my schedule and did not know where the rooms were. I was frantic and frustrated that they only had one woman at registration. I was drunk. I felt out of control and ashamed. Then I was trying to make coffee in a house and the crock pot was mixed in with the coffee. The woman who had been drinking with me was there that morning. I was saying we have to be careful when we drink. All of a sudden, George appeared. He was young and strong. Suddenly I felt tremendous safety and love. He had gone somewhere and missed me and wanted to come back to me. I was so grateful. I felt renewed.

Comment: George helped me get sober.

4/18 Pulling together a gathering of black people mostly men. Preparing brown envelopes with papers and perhaps pins - symbolic, maybe flags. Then everything went into chaos and violence. The attendees went on a destructive rampage. A black woman had a gun with pins in it. I followed her into the restroom. I was holding my right arm up so that the pins would hit my arm. Waiting for pain. She flew up to the top of the stall. I was in the open door. No pain.

Inside a spiritual store or office. My bike was stolen. Nobody cared. I had four plastic packages of cannabis in my purse. I was going to the tip of Manhattan for French. I crossed between a bike and a car. I had to pay two dollars to cross the street. I started up steep stairs with a bike. Two men grabbed my purse and pulled the pot out. Were they Chinese? They were exposing me - telling people around us. I grabbed it back and started up the hill again. I was worried whether I would make it.

Comment: Gratuitous violence pervades my life. Nowhere is safe.

3/19/18 I was supposed to be at a class to learn about my senior paper. I climbed up the hill to another building for my class. Like another dream where the classes are in a separate building, Paterson, Newark, and you must go down the street a long way. I got to the building, but no one knew about the class. I tried to call the administration but there was no answer. I was panic-stricken and sad. Then coming back down the hill, I saw a bear on another hill coming down. I climbed up an old fire escape. He was trying to bite me and I was kicking him off with my feet. Hanging on for dear life to a pole. Dennis woke me up.

Comment: My fears are chasing me.

5/27/18 I was volunteering to talk to mental health professionals about the rape. My therapist was encouraging me. I was rushed, self-conscious and wearing my nightgown. The room was full of people. I was telling them how devastating it was to be raped. I said something about terror and then a large black cloud and deep darkness. We went to another meeting of health professionals and they read the case study but did not want to hear me talk. The male doctors said 'sad and interesting' and walked out.

Comment: Rape is not understood unless experienced.

7/4/18 I was in a school where there was a stabbing. We were putting up barriers to keep the perpetrator out. I was scared. George was there. I said, 'you left me.' Malinda was near. She said nothing happened. Hank colored his hair orange. Had he become a clown?

7/25/18 Pat, my former therapist, was accusing and humiliating me. We were in a dissertation class and I tried to present my ideas. She was accusing me of being high and of getting plastered several days before. I kept crying that I am clean and sober for 8 years. The other women were confused and sided with Pat. Some of them had pot in their bags. Why did Pat not want me in that school? I had another PhD. She clearly hated me.

Comment: The shame and guilt of alcoholism linger long after sobriety.

12/26/19 Dream: An intern was observing me doing psychotherapy. She resembled a current client, tall, thin, brunette. A client came with a complex history and was talking about sexual abuse. The intern tried to interrupt, and I shut her down. She started crying in her hands, head down. When I asked, 'Are you ok?' she erupted and then reported me to the evaluators for ignoring her. This was my house, a large kitchen, and dirty dishes from dozens of guests. The white women were criticizing me saying I had confronted them and was angry. They would evaluate me. I was saying you do not understand. I started cleaning up thinking,' No good deed goes unpunished.'

Comment: I can never get my own life into order.

Descending into Dreams

Helen of Troy, the most beautiful woman in the world according to Paris, was twins with Cassandra, a Trojan Princess. Cassandra, who was brought back to Greece by Agamemnon after the Greeks defeated Troy in a decade-long war, foresaw that the Greeks would kill her if she entered the palace, and so she went forward to her death. She was credited with the gift of foresight, the ability to tell the future. The Jungians believe that dreams have the power to tell the future.

I have always valued my dreams and looked for meaning in them. According to the dream interpretation process of Dr. Carl Jung called 'amplification', we look at the symbols first because they are pointing to the archetypes. We can then ask ourselves what does this symbol evoke? First, we search for memories in our own lives and associations from our personal experiences. Then we look for the symbol in the seminal narratives that inform our lives such as novels, movies, ancient myths, folk tales, stories from history, heroes and heroines. The Jungian analyst needs to have knowledge of myth and folklore from different traditions and can then help to call that association to mind in service of unearthing the client's unconscious material. Often the analyst finds that the client is living a narrative found in folklore.

All the Cinderellas, all the Snow Whites, all the Roman and Greek goddesses are repeating their stories through us. The narrative becomes bigger and better; we are becoming courageous and enlightened. We are the heroes and heroines. When the analyst can identify the story, the client awakens as if from a dream. The client enters the truth of the narrative, which is Joseph Campbell's hero journey. Amplification of the dream and the waking life allows the story to drive the life to this fated conclusion.

One of my mentors was Robert Moss, a neo-Jungian who has dedicated his lifetime to dreams. In his experience, dreams serve a variety of purposes including connection with symbols and through them to the archetypal material in the collective unconscious. These symbols that conjure our ancestral legacies in our personal unconscious offer us gifts. These gifts descend the genetic cline into our consciousness when we explore the legacy of our parents, grandparents, and so forth who are present with their skills, their characteristics, their stories. The ancestors, as pioneers in previous generations, perpetuate through the bloodline the culture in which we live and the land on which we stand. Women of power manifest through our courage and perseverance. Entanglement with the land on which we live brings forth the ancient cultures and the animal spirits. The Lake Huron seagulls, the Calusa Indians in Bokeelia, Florida, the mule deer on the Colorado land are my friends. We also have connections to places where we travel. Malinda is still in Paris awaiting me. The Cathars and French Huguenots in the South of France are calling me.

Another primal purpose of dreams is to foretell the future; Jung believed that dreams are teleological; the answer to the question 'why?' requires patience to allow the future to reveal itself. Healing can also be enabled as the dream identifies the areas of weakness in the body and moves aside the rigid defenses that maintain the disease state, allowing the natural healing process in the body to be unleashed. As we dream into the past, we find the lost pieces of ourSelves and identify where the soul's energy has been fixated in the stages of development. Then we can heal that inner child, that disillusioned teen, that ambitious young adult, that depressed and addicted adult who lost all hope during the journey of life.

We also can gain a better perspective as the witness of our own actions so that the conscience or superego can emerge from repressed material to make corrections in the way our lives have unfolded. I have found in the hypnagogic state at the edge of wakening that my regrets surface from repression. At times I can make amends. Most recently, I reviewed all the regrets from my retirement and departure from the NJ Department of Human Services. My anxiety had been crippling and alienated people I respected. How to make amends to people I cannot find? How to thank them for all the support they offered?

***

Oh, nobly born. You are the Buddha awakening. Quiet the mind. Tend to the heart. Escape the Duka, the 10,000 joys and 10,000 sorrows. Stay in the state of deep sleep where the world is an illusion, and the dream of the Pure Lands of the Buddha is the paradise you seek. Indeed, the awakening state after sleep, hypnagogia, is believed to contain the most powerful dreams and the most easily recalled because they occur right at the cusp of awakening.

The experiences of this state are descending, heavy, replete with free association, containing no boundaries, no space, no time and no body. The desire to wander in the terrain of the Pure Lands surrounded by healing herbs, yellow butterflies and sacred mandalas is strong. One delays the inevitable onslaught of worldly life. After residing in the Pure Lands, one must return to samsara the Place of Suffering, so as not to forget.

My very first recurring dream from childhood revealed its meaning. A fox was chasing me on a path, and I was deathly afraid of being caught. I slipped down off the path to hide and was clinging with my hands to the edge of a bridge. The fox was nipping at my fingers. A psychoanalyst interpreted the fox as my father. In dream reentry, I surrendered to the river below. I let go and stopped running in fear. Then I became the fox with alert bright eyes, white, black, and auburn fur; he is a part of me. I tamed the fox as did The Little Prince. I climbed my soul tree to the highest branches and saw the river of my life; I was told to go forward; then the fox and I flew or climbed the spires of Chartres Cathedral into the spiritual dimension, and we flowed down the Garonne into the Mediterranean Sea. The fox was not my father; he was myself. I had tamed the fox as did *Le Petit Prince*, the Little Prince of Antoine de Saint Exupéry.

My dreams of departed ones became vivid, memorable, and frequent. The dead have a pact with the living. They have not left us for good and all. We can find them in nature, active imagination, and dreams. I dream of the dead, departed loved ones. They want us to tell their stories and to forgive them for leaving.

Bel Canto by Ann Patchett

"He wondered now if everyone had a private life. It was possible that all those years he had been alone, never knowing that a complete world existed, and no one spoke of it. As much as he was overwhelmed by love, he could never really shake what he knew to be true; that every night they were together could be seen as a miracle for one hundred different reasons, not the least of which was that at some point these days would end."

Both Hank and Malinda, two of my twins in life, come back to tell their story, to get the story straight, to clarify details and see their lives as they truly were. Both prefer to see themselves through my eyes, my memories and my visions. They trust me to tell their stories with all respect, sacredness, and truth. I truly knew them and accepted them as they truly were. My Tao master says that this is a gift that we are given in life – to be known. Thus, they return to me because I will tell the truth.

Dreams about Malinda

My dreams of Malinda are filled with love and loss. She is standing beside me, helping me, rising to higher levels, and often outshining me. The water is turbulent or still, whatever the state of my unconsciousness on that day or in that dream. We are packing and leaving. My parents are no help, ineffective, passive. My other sisters are distant.

07/03/08 I was supposed to waitress. My dog was with me and I needed to take her home. At home, some men were there who were vying for another younger woman. Was it Malinda? I was feeling rejected and very alone. I had been interested in one of the men. I went to the door and said to a woman there, 'I always lose out on the men because they want Malinda, and otherwise they think we are freaks. Malinda slept with one of my guys, but we were too young to know any better.' Then I went to the restaurant. There were two long tables filled and two waitresses. I was confused about my role. I asked, 'Do we usually have three waitresses?' and she said, 'Yes, on Saturday night.' Again, I was the odd man out.

8/5/08 In truth, that day I was diagnosed with cancer in the right breast. In the dream, I gave Hank to Malinda. They loved each other and they were far away from me. I went to them and asked for inclusion. They looked at each other with love and understanding and did not make room for me. I realized that it was too late. They did not need me anymore.

Comment: They were both dead, and I was not destined to die from breast cancer, although I did not realize that then. On 8/14, I was sitting in a sauna trying to cure the cancer when I thought that someone was wanting me dead, perhaps my mother. My maternal grandmother had four daughters, and two of them died before their mother. Is history repeating itself? Am I destined to go through unprocessed emotional territory? Are these unfelt emotions that have fallen to me? Has the energy been stuck all this time? I must use insight and compassion.

03/01/10 Climbing up stairs to different levels with pools. Malinda and John were too busy; they were visiting. A man with them came over – actually I approached him, and he sat with me trying to kiss me, rough and big. I thought,' Can I like this?' He said, 'I am getting nowhere with you.'

We went to an apartment on the ground floor. There were games on that floor near the ocean. A pool. A man said a lot of people are coming for a conference and I said,' They will enjoy the water even if it is cool.' The woman in the apartment wanted to chat. Outside some gals said, 'Is that your sister? Why is she not with you?' I replied, 'She is too busy with John and he hates me.' In the kitchen Mal was beautiful with long dark hair, but impassive. John ignored me and I him – passing as if we never met. He had no face. The other man, their friend, was getting something out of a cupboard. He was friendly but distant.

A young girl was sitting with her mother. They showed pictures and talked about when the brother almost died. I said, 'Many have had experiences when we almost died. That is important.' I had long dark hair like Malinda, but she was gorgeous. I did not know if I was pretty in her shadow.

5/10/11 I am going on a journey with Malinda. I am going to learn French. I wonder if I can truly learn so well now, but I want to stay current and active and to keep trying and breaking through to new worlds.

05/12/11 Malinda and I were getting married on the same day. After the reception I must have blacked out on whiskey and killed her. I was trying to remember how I had killed her – stabbing? I did not remember. We were all camping at Lake Huron. I went to Anne and Al. I was so guilty and knew they were afraid and disgusted. I tried so hard to be good. Al kept asking me to get water. He gave me a plastic holder with many holes. I walked down to the water edge and brought back about two cups. He laughed and I threw the water in his face. Then Harry and I went to get more, and I took Al's horse. The water edge became a cave overhanging. The horse stood up and became a man. He introduced himself as a wild western man. We got water and headed back. I had the reins.

Later I was walking out of the cave with Harry, and he was asking me what I had to do if I only had 48 days of sobriety. Wasn't there a requirement for x number of meetings? I did not remember. I said, ``Is this all the sobriety I have?' They reminded me of the night after the reception when I had a bottle of whiskey in my hand. I could see myself in my mind's eye but could not remember in life that I would do that. Why? It did not seem right.

Anne was two Annes, the placid impassive older one and the young one, maybe four. She was still collecting data for her dissertation. I told Al that my dissertation had been quick and short – minimal – to get through the doctorate, and I was still called PhD – no reason to be the smartest person on the planet.

02/10/12 A large group ready to go on a hike/climb/quest. Sacred objects everywhere. A cavernous room like a cave. An Indian woman gave me a sacred object to take. I was honored. A god or goddess perhaps. We were going up a trail, climbing the back wall of the cave.

Comment: I am using sacred magic to find Hank and Malinda. I was a twin, and I woke up alone.

4/17/12 Last night I had a very real and intense dream about Malinda. We were in Paris. She was fluent in French, and she was taking me around to find an apartment. Mal was vibrant, very alive, very real. She was happy in Paris, beautiful, competent, at home.

4/20/14 I am starting a new store. A former partner and I were assembling posters that I had somehow made. My father was asleep, and my mother was saying, 'be quiet, do not wake your father.' This former partner was a caricature with red hair, long pointy nose, eating pastries, pacing, growling. Malinda and John were supposed to help me but were too busy packing as usual.

Then my hair had conditioner. I was in my bathrobe walking down the street. I went to join the meditation class, and they were planning coffee. Their rooms were across from my store. I wanted to join them, but I was not dressed. I realized I was alone with my project, no help, no interest. I was frightened and still determined.

Comment: I am alone without Malinda. John has taken her from me and she was killed in a plane. Since she met John, they are always packing and leaving me in the dreams.

08/03/14 I dreamt many people in my family had died. Two young children. Perhaps Olivia and Winnie. (Now I realize they were my mother's two young sisters when she was young.) Then Malinda. I was with John, trying to comfort each other. Anne and Al had excluded me from the preparations. I was very angry. Then my grandfather died. A woman was volunteering with me and she got involved with my sisters to attend a funeral. I was excluded again.

Comment: After Malinda died, I was excluded from many family events.

When I had cancer, I thought that someone was wanting me dead and probably my mother. Her mother had four daughters, and two died before she did. Is history repeating itself? I fooled them. I was cured.

10/29/14 I was flying in a small plane out of Teterboro. I was going perhaps to the cottage to see my mother. A large airliner passed too near and the pilot stared at me. I got very tired and landed. I needed rest. I could not make it that far.

11/25/14 Malinda and I were flying to Europe. I only had x amount of cash and I knew it was not enough. I kept thinking we will get more travelers checks when we get there. We were walking around in an airport and then we separated for our flights. Malinda went towards a different flight.

02/22/15 Last night Malinda was in my dream. We were finishing our final papers for college. On the paper, she got A+. I got an A -. There were Egyptian hieroglyphs and they led into esoteric spiritual information. The teacher thought it odd. Another girl, tall and large, also got an A+. I knew her and I knew they were smarter than I. Piles of books and trying to integrate them into a whole paper. A den surrounded with books.

04/16/15 Many people with us, Malinda there, all planning to go to a retreat. My mother was there. I wanted to go on the train. Malinda and I had gone on the train before. Others were driving. I could not find the phone reservation number. I tried my phone, the phone book, and the security at the complex. Malinda was not helping. Then I decided to get Hank. He was flirting with his prior girlfriend. I pulled him out of the room. He disappeared into a small box with only his face. I screamed, 'Come out!' and I was trying to claw him but could not move my hands. I screamed, 'You think I am capable and normal, but sometimes I am paralyzed.' I could not get my hands out of the sleeves. Raging. Scared. Woke up struggling in the bed.

5/24/16 There was a place where people came to dance and meet each other. Malinda was dressed up and she could play the violin. I was casual and sat up in the corner. She came to join me, and we sat together watching the others arrive and mingle. Then we went to a mall to get something to eat. I knew a restaurant, but we did not stay. A man came up to us and said we had very unusual eyes. He could use us to hypnotize other people. We agreed.

1/5/17 My father was packing the car. Anne and Al were there at my house in Harmon Cove. We had decided to leave that day, but we were waiting for Bob. I said "Al, call Bob so that he does not have to come all this way."

Malinda was lying on the carport with me. An old friend came up and pretended to be someone else. I was tending to the plants. I was wearing heels and a skirt hitting a tennis ball against a wall and then I could not do it. A man was playing tennis with me remotely. I said I will come back when I have the proper outfit.

1/25/18 Malinda and I were preparing for a play in French. We put on the skirts that our mother had prepared for the Cottage Capades, in which Malinda and I performed a gypsy dance, but mine was too long. We needed to memorize the lines in French. I was furious at Anne because she lent the French dictionary to a friend and did not get it back. I did not know the words. Then I was screaming at mom and dad because they did not help us. I was screaming that they were not proper parents. Dennis woke me up. I was afraid to fail and be exposed.

2018 I hugged Malinda between me and another person. She was wearing blue. Then I told them she had been killed in a car accident, but I was not sure. John, Anne and Catherine were with me cleaning out Malinda's dorm room. She had died. A woman took her diary and I claimed it back. I knew that she had written something profound, and I was looking for it. We separated the clothes and some pants that were originally mine.

My mother was taking care of my grandmother, who looked noticeably young. She had studded glasses, and I borrowed them to go out on a bike in the streets of London. I realized that I had no addresses or phone numbers and could not return. I was wandering in stores looking for the bike. Then I bit off the tips of the glasses and tried to use them anyway. I was hopelessly lost.

No date: Someone, either myself or Malinda, had engaged in a serious offense for which amends were necessary. The offense related to John Efroymson, who had convinced her to take a trip and bypass someone waiting. My mother was packing up a house filled with memorabilia. Books, stars, dolls everywhere I looked. I was more beautiful. She was scattered as usual. Malinda could not join us unless she expressed remorse. Did she truly accept what she had done?

Comment: She had been convinced to fly to Montreal that day, and she never expected to die. A high price to pay.

4/1/20 We were collecting Malinda's belongings. My mother was helping. A young guy had them and was insisting that we take them all. I had a small sports car and kept saying we cannot take the big comforter. Give them away to the thrift store. Then my mother would insist that we take them home.

She had made bags full of comforters, jewelry, so much stuff. Why did we need it?

"So," I said, "I will do two trips." Then the car would not start. The gay men were high and partying. We were sitting in small groups and I was trying my best to be accepted and useful. It all seemed like wasted effort and trivial.

5/17/20 At the cottage with waves pounding on the shore, Mal was there helping me pack to leave. I was very tired, and my clothes were a mess.

Mom and Anne were in the kitchen. I was thinking, 'I will sleep and then leave at dawn.' I told an aunt or mom's friend that I would rather see what I am passing by in the car. Ted Todd was looking at me very directly out back of the cottage. Harry was behind him watching. I said, 'Ted, just hug me,' and he did. He rubbed a hard-on. I wandered to where children were playing, exceedingly small girl twins. I held one and I could not tell if she had any arms. The parents came for them and put them in shoe boxes for the ride. They had many children.

5/20/20 My colleagues at work were all at a conference where we were getting final information about finances for the men. One woman gave me hair dye, and my hair was transformed into white with colorful squiggles and short unruly bangs. I was going downstairs to show everyone. Malinda and another woman were in an elevator where we just talked oblivious to the floor we had reached. When we went into the big room, I became blind to everyone and disoriented. I thought I was going to bump into someone.

Then Malinda led me to a seat on a banquet raised above the crowd. She had her right arm around me on my left holding me secure. I said, 'Can we scoot back a little. I feel like I am going to fall off.' We did. I was self-conscious with my hair.

Comment: Malinda is showing me the upper world. I am an angel with white hair.

The Preparation

The heroine who is capable of descending to the underworld, confronting physical death, surviving despair, needs a strong start in life. She needs to know that she is hand-picked for extraordinary feats of courage and daring. She needs to know that she has the skills and aptitudes, the genetics, the lineage and family support, the intelligence, and emotional power to overcome all challenges. Perhaps she will be born a twin and know that she is so special and so gifted that she is unstoppable.

Achieving Proficiency

The goddess Styx had twin sons. Prometheus created humans and gave them fire against the will of Zeus. Epimetheus, his brother, created animals. Zeus was seeking vengeance and so he created Pandora to marry the brother with the gift of curiosity and gave her a box with the instruction 'do not open.' Pandora opened the box and let out all evil. When she opened the box the second time, out came hope.

Diana and Apollo were twins born to Leda and Zeus. In true form Hera became enraged by Zeus' infidelity and banished Leda from Mount Olympus to be exiled on a remote island. There Leda birthed the twins, first Diana who then helped with the birth of Apollo. Diana and Apollo are the most pertinent of all the yin/yang figures in Roman mythology; Diana is identified with the moon and Apollo with the Sun. They were extremely proficient archers and defended their mother viciously. Diana was a huntress who lived alone with the animals and only hunted for food. Apollo became a beautiful God admired by all for his brightness and courage.

After an idyllic childhood filled with twin joys, one might wonder what would come next. A solid foundation of proficiency in many skills and intellectual pursuits was the next goal for the twins. Our parents opened doors for us, that is true, but we were the children who bravely marched through them. We were avid readers, good at schoolwork; we loved learning. We took three years of French and five years of Latin, which prepared us for our later language achievements. We were candidates at Girls State, leaders of the Junior Women's Clubs, Honor Roll every term. We also played many sports and excelled in them. I was the right wing on the field hockey team.

Did this foreshadow Malinda's death when the right wing of her plane collapsed onto her, crushing her? Malinda was a guard and I was a rover on the basketball team. We played tennis; I was undefeated all four years of high school and still have the little trophy to show for this feat. Malinda was a member of the National Honor Society, which I did not attain because I did not take the extra credit courses. This was a huge and unexpected consequence of my course choices. My mother begged the school to reconsider, but they refused.

A few other notable events helped our formation. Malinda and I both continued studying Latin in high school with Dr. Otto through our fifth year. We were also taking French. By that final year, we were reading the Iliad and the Odyssey about the stealing of Helen of Troy from Athens, the subsequent Trojan War, the heroic struggle between Achilles and Hector, the fall of Troy, and the wandering of Ulysses. We were familiar with Romulus and Remus, the myths of Greek and Roman culture, the gods and goddesses. Heroes and heroines were our friends. We lived in an archetypal world with Dr. Otis, exploring the grand sweep of myth and history, the great battles, the suicide of the queen Diana on her funeral pyre in Carthage. Latin also helped me translate other romance languages, and so when Malinda and I spent our Junior Year in Paris, we were already linguists.

Twin studies have indicated a high correlation in skills and aptitudes within identical twin pairs, perhaps as high as 65% The IQ correlation is very high, almost 85 to 90%. We had apparently inherited our father's intellectual ability. He had memorized Shakespeare and won all his legal cases; clearly his mental abilities had been passed down. My mother had graduated from Smith College, which was a feat coming from a hamlet such as Cincinnati, Ohio. No doubt she contributed some DNA to our intellectual success.

Strangely, however, the twins' interests were also very close. We both ended by studying languages in college and taking our Junior Year abroad. Malinda had been the memory keeper all along the journey and I was worried that I would forget my childhood or my studies. I counted on her to support me in all my courses and projects, so the prospect of separation was bleak. There began to be parts of her life that I did not share and parts of my experience that she did not know.

Malinda and I had already decided that we would go to separate colleges. I was accepted to Goucher College in Towson, MD on an early decision and Malinda chose Wells College in Aurora, NY. Wells College, a small enclave in the NY Finger-lakes, was nestled near Ithaca, Colgate, Cornell, so the intellectual stimulation was high.

For the first time we were going to live apart. This phase of our lives was extremely challenging because we only wanted to be with people who knew us as twins. We did not evoke the same awe and fascination by separating. I remember telling everyone at Goucher that I was a twin. We both wanted to attend all girl schools so that we could more readily focus on our studies. The high school competition for boyfriends and popularity had exhausted us.

Malinda and I spent our Junior Year in France with Sweet Briar College. Back in those days, studying abroad meant spending one whole academic year there. Malinda generated the idea and I hitchhiked onto the trip at the last minute. Sweet Briar was happy to have me, but apparently Malinda did not feel the same. She wanted to succeed in an area that I had not yet invaded. There are incomplete memories with my twin Malinda from our junior year with Sweet Briar in Paris during 1968/9, one of the most memorable years of our lives.

The Vietnam War was the backdrop and Richard Nixon defeated Hubert Humphrey in the Presidential election. In Paris, 'les evenements de mai' (the events of May) had left their mark. Students and workers had rebelled against an aristocratic society, marching in the streets and escaping into the bowels of the subway. Unrest sparked frequently that fall, and we learned to avoid the tear gas. We read the Herald Tribune daily, devouring the news from the US and the world. We studied theater at Reid Hall, the center where American students gathered, and attended plays in the grand venues of Paris.

When Dennis, my current partner, said that when he saw the Goucher College yearbook he observed that it depicted a luxurious protected world of excellence and that it must have changed my life. Indeed, it did. I was immersed in cultural studies: French literature, Paris, Louvre, plays such as Ubu Roi, The Chairs, Racine, Corneille, Puce à l'Oreille, Jeu de Paume, Eiffel Tower, Metro, Musee d'Orsay.

I fell in love with the Seine, the Left Bank, the Diary of Anais Nin, the cafes, Doris Lessing, and the Existentialists: John Paul Sartre, Simone de Beauvoir, Alfred Camus, and Samuel Becket. I read the novels of Simone de Beauvoir, Sartre's paramour. We devoured their philosophy of absolute freedom and the absurdity of life coupled with full responsibility. We saw the plays *Ubu Roi, No Exit,* and *Waiting for Godot* in famous theater houses. We read *The Plague* and *The Stranger* by Camus, seminal in my thinking. In the *Plague,* some people in the quarantine town (a metaphor for earth), where all will die, are passive and simply await death. Others try to heal. I already knew which I would be.

I resonated with Hegel, a German Romantic Idealist, b. 1770 who philosophized that history is a dialectic struggle that brings about progressive synthesis and the evolution of humanity. The Absolute Idea runs through all Being and all Truth. Sadly, his philosophy contributed to Nazism. Sartre had studied his philosophy in Berlin, as well as the work of Martin Heidegger and Frederik Nietzsche, both precursors of Existentialism. Frederik Nietzsche in his *Genealogy of Morals* stressed that the ripest fruit is the sovereign individual who is autonomous and liberated from custom. He has the will to power, responsibility and conscience; and he has victory over God and nothingness/meaninglessness.

Jean Paul Sartre (1905-1980) captured and imprisoned by the Nazis in 1940, created the model of Existentialism: no excuses, no recourse, only freedom, no god, no divine plan, no universal morality or law. Our moral worth lies in our relationship to our freedom and the freedom of others. Our 'facticity,' -a prior limits, dictates our fundamental situation, which we transcend by refusing the limits of authority drawn from civilization and the age. Can you even imagine a young woman of 19 uncovering these powerful truths?

That year Malinda and I spent essentially apart because we had boyfriends who took our attention away from each other. During the holidays, my boyfriend John Aniello and I traveled through Spain, Italy, and Morocco.

Gordon Chase, an artist who wore his hair in an odd long smooth cap with swirling bangs, kept Malinda occupied. I did not realize until that spring how fragile Malinda really was outside of the twin norms. A man who befriended her came to our bedroom and stole some francs that our mother had sent, and this was a matter of guilt and obsession for her. When Gordon broke off their relationship, she must have plummeted into depression and did not tell me.

In the spring, I had entered a hospital for vaginal bleeding and had my hands full during this term with my course work. I did not have extra energy to devote to Malinda even though we lived in the same room in the 18th Arrondissement near the Arc de Triomphe. We had no concept of mental illness back then and I would not have recognized a complex of symptoms. I was not attuned. Malinda dropped out of all her courses and did not finish that semester. I persevered, took my final exam -mostly oral in French- and completed. My parents later blamed me for her downfall. I do not understand to this day what I could have done to prevent this or treat it. She needed to be in psychotherapy and on medication, which carried a severe stigma back then. The Sweet Briar staff were the ones responsible for observing this depression and getting her help. I was not an adult.

My boyfriend John Aniello was very supportive during this time. We remained partners through the next year when he returned to Yale and I to Goucher. Malinda also had dear friends from Paris at Yale, Byron Gross as an example, and we both visited our Paris companions the following year at Yale. Meanwhile, Malinda shared that she was tripping on LSD and talking to me in the mirror. I left John after college because I was not mature enough to get married and move to Hartford, Connecticut, where he would manage his father's automotive business.

My mother attacked me much later in life with the alleged truth that Malinda had not wanted me to go to Paris at all. This cruel remark came after Malinda's death and I wondered why, if Malinda felt this way, did she not confide in me. I could have stayed at Goucher. I eventually concluded that my mother was exaggerating in order to make herself more important. She was jealous of my bond with Malinda. My parents magically believed that in most circumstances I was responsible for protecting Malinda, the weaker twin. My parents remained disappointed in me. My sisters Anne and Catherine took this opportunity to get closer to Malinda and transcend my influence. To this day, they fantasize that they know Malinda better than I do. The truth is this: no siblings will ever penetrate the Twin World. This is their greatest frustration.

Malinda returned to Haddonfield, rejoined our nuclear family and finished the lost semester at Gloucester College. The following year, after I had graduated from Goucher College cum laude with a BA in French Literature, she returned to Wells College and completed her degree, studying French and Italian. She continued to have emotional challenges including the theft of her valuable notebook. She was offered a Woodrow Wilson fellowship to study French and Italian but did not feel strong enough to accept. They waived her final exams because she had lost her study material, and Malinda graduated with high honors. Like our father, she had a very high cognitive intelligence and a strong work ethic.

Because I had moved through college one year earlier and become a VISTA Volunteer in Philadelphia that next year, I had left the family behind in some wonderful way. I knew Malinda was safe. I came home occasionally, but I had moved on. Perhaps I sensed that my parents still believed I had been selfish in not rescuing Malinda from her breakdown in Paris. Perhaps I could not fit into my mother's projections of the Bad Twin.

During the Seventies, Malinda came back to confer with me after a stint in VISTA in Washington, DC, in order to determine her future. Bob Gorman and I had relocated to a beautiful little cottage in West Yarmouth near his old haunts in Hyannis on Cape Cod. Bob had grown up in Watertown, so the Cape was his summer 'go to.' Malinda decided to get her master's degree in learning disabilities, a new field back then due to recent breakthroughs with the brain. She met John Efroymson at my house, when he was looking for a tennis partner. They moved back to Washington, DC. where John and Malinda both taught in elementary schools. Then they moved to a sheep farm in Northern Virginia. They took one year to drive a minibus around Europe and North Africa. Malinda was raped by tribal desert men in Morocco. Both she and John believed they would be killed. Many years later Malinda told me about this trauma. I listened with the empathy of a rape victim and never mentioned it again. I do not know if she ever told anyone else in the family; I doubt it.

Bob and I had visited them one weekend in Northern Virginia where they were both teaching. I still had full-blown PTSD from my experience with rape. If I would find myself in a small space, a car, or a stairwell, I experienced claustrophobia from that original stairwell and would scream at people, including Bob. Bob understood the aftermath of rape. Malinda sadly decided to believe that I was not a good person towards Bob and refused to go out to dinner with me. I cried and hallucinated all night long until they put me on the train to Newark. I was devastated. I do not know if I ever recovered from that blow.

Malinda and John decided to relocate to Ithaca, New York where John had a nest of friends from his time at Purdue University. The Finger Lakes area where Malinda had attended college at Wells was near many universities such as Cornell, Colgate, and Ithaca College; the community was filled with intellectual stimulation for both. Their friends were artisans and politically avant garde; in fact they were Democratic Socialists in the main.

In the Eighties they had a program produced in Ithaca, *More than the News*. Mal was the star and interviewer. The program emphasized local news in Ithaca with actions that one could take to be part of the solution. Malinda became famous in the community. Her picture was on the back of buses, and people revered her contribution to bettering society.

At this point, I found out from Malinda that John was distancing from her. She was still experiencing his withdrawal when they flew with their friends to Montreal. Perhaps she had decided to leave this world. The Taoist masters can choose the moment of their death and ascend through the crown chakra into the spiritual body, which they had projected for this purpose using the microcosmic orbit and the pearl.

The Miraculous Birth

Athena (Minerva) was born to Zeus alone. She sprang from his head full grown and ready for battle. In the Iliad she is a fierce battle goddess, a protectress of the city of Athens, of civilized life, of handicrafts, and agriculture. She tames horses for humans to use. Her temple was the

Parthenon, the olive, her tree, the owl, her bird. She is the most powerful of all the virgin goddesses. Zeus trusts her to carry his most potent weapon, his thunderbolt.

After Leda the Swan was banished from Olympus by Hera, Zeus' wife, to a small island Delos for consorting with Zeus, she bore twin children: Diana and Apollo. In the myth Diana is born first and helps her birth Apollo. Within weeks they are full grown. They have prodigious proficiency in archery and are ready to defend their mother with their bows and arrows. Dianna is the goddess of the moon. She both hunts and protects animals, especially the sacred deer. Her twin brother Apollo is the god of light and truth. His oracle at Delphi was considered the center of the world, and people from every area came to consult her. Apollo taught men the healing arts. Seen as a purely beneficent power he helped humans make peace with the Gods. Apollo taught humanity how to achieve redemption from the gravest deeds.

Romulus and Remus, born of Mars and Rhea Silva, grandnephews of King Amulus of Alba Longa, are abandoned on the River Tiber, so as not to threaten the established ruler with their bloodline. They are suckled by a She-Wolf who saves their lives. The shepherd Faustulus finds them and raises them. The twins found a city called Rome around 750 BC. Different stories are told about Remus' death; one portrays his death as an accident at the hand of his brother, and another attributes his death to a dispute over the hill on which Rome would be founded. The Greeks landed in Sicily as early as the 8th Century BC, and Aeneas is also credited with founding Rome after the Trojan War. The Louvre contains a beautiful statue of the twins suckling from the She-Wolf and the god of the River Tiber watching over the scene.

Malinda and I stood at the portal branching into two alternate realities.

We passed through effortlessly and gladly with the conviction that our hearts were joined. We knew that all our chakras were open to spiritual ascension. We knew that we would experience a quality of love that would transform our souls and everyone on Earth that we touched. We knew that other twin souls awaited us and that we would meet them on the path. That we would live in a Twin World with them and that singles would not understand the bond that we had made at the portal.

The Neptune quality of the womb was our first earthly experience, and then 'lo and behold' we were separated from one egg into two. As the Tao was one and then two. As the watery dark chaos of the World was separated into Heaven and Earth. Then two souls came down at 18 weeks and occupied the split egg. Many decisions were hatched in that world as we discussed our intention for this lifetime. Who would be born first? Who would take the lead later? What strengths would we share, and which would we divide between us? What archetypes would be activated? What exact date and time would we choose for birth and where would the planets be? How would we manifest the Yin and Yang?

Two twin daughters were born in 1948, May 23, under the sun sign of Gemini, The Twins. We were Air Signs destined to be smart, mercurial, communicative, and fascinated by life. The sun appears in the 7th house, the house of partnership and mirroring. With Scorpio rising, we had numerous secrets between us, and we had intensive desires. This deep and meaningful relationship with each other was assured. Chiron the wounded healer occupies the first house. The development of the self happens for us in Scorpio. Chiron here would indicate that a wound will occur that cannot be cured, and the individual must accept the permanent wound within the first house of the journey. The moon is in the first house in Sagittarius, indicating a deep desire to undertake an independent journey of philosophical exploration. This self-searching would manifest meaningful ventures in life. Jupiter, the most expansive of signs, also appears in Sagittarius in the second house. Jupiter points towards self-worth and one's own assets, signifying a propensity towards optimism and growth.

The eighth house signals family secrets, inheritance and death. Venus, the greatest desire, appears in Cancer, who promotes love of family, in the 8th house where deep and perhaps dark events occur. Furthermore, a conjunction between Mercury and Uranus in Gemini in the 8th house might indicate sudden change and perhaps death. Gemini is an air sign characterized by intelligence, elevated thoughts and higher education. Gemini is ruled by Mercury the messenger. Could we even say a sudden death in the air?

Our fire signs predominate with two planets appearing in Leo, the extrovert and the leader: Saturn indicating hard work to achieve the prize, and Pluto the life and death struggle to transform. The combination of Saturn and Pluto in the 9th house of spirituality and philosophy influences us to bury the old-world views, in order to transform the collective consciousness. Mars, the doer and actor, appears in Virgo, the organized and detailed force, in the 10th house, the public persona, indicating a successful career. Neptune is in Libra in the 11th house, amplifying idealization, redemption, collective ideals and optimism. An auspicious chart generally except for the 8th house cluster of Uranus (sudden upheaval) Mercury (the wings of change) and Venus (the most beautiful of all.)

Our mother Margery Sisson Runyan came from an old family, owners of the paper mill in Potsdam New York. One Sisson brother, her father Lewis Hamilton Sisson, was sent to the Queen City Cincinnati to join the banking industry because there were too many brothers for them all to run the mill. We had reams of paper in our basement for years when I was young on Pleasant Street in Mariemont, Ohio. My mother's mother, Margaret Parker Sisson, was an organist at the First Presbyterian Church when she met Lewis in Potsdam. As a pianist she could play by ear. She befriended artists in the symphony orchestra when she was not driving down to Mexico in her big Cadillac and bringing back religious artifacts hidden in her suitcase. Four girls were born to the Sisson family in Hyde Park in Cincinnati: only two survived.

Our mother went to Smith College and found herself shipped out of Europe where she and her sister Mary Louise went to study when World War II began. Our father was a lawyer, Phi Beta Kappa from Ohio Wesleyan and Cornell Law. He worked with the Taft law firm and later Kroger, RCA, NCR as a labor law expert on the management side. He argued many times before the National Labor Relations Board and rarely lost a case. The twins were the first born in a successful family system. Our names were in the Blue Book of Cincinnati. How could we be anything but extraordinary?

PICTURE OF GRANDPARENTS, PARENTS, AND TWINS

I have realized from my mother's story of our conception and birth, and many client histories over the 15 years of psychotherapy, that the narrative of these events is seminal in the projection on the child. My mother's repetitive and committed story began with unprotected sex with my father, the loss of her job at IBM doing training on business machines, the horrible and lonely birth. 'I was on my own,' the postpartum exhaustion. My grandmother hired a nurse to care for us. Benjamin Spock had inculcated her generation to only feed infants on a schedule. She suffered through our crying, believing herself unable to help us. This narrative created a reality that twins are difficult. Naturally, we had our own language and did not bond so readily with adult caregivers because we had the strongest bond with each other.

We wanted to do everything alike: look alike, dress alike, study the same subjects in the same classrooms. The schools separated us in elementary school, but we rejoined in high school.

We lived in a small house on Beech Street in Mariemont, an upscale suburb of Cincinnati, until we moved to Pleasant Street near the Carillon tower and the huge park with baseball fields. When the Carillon tower rang it was our signal to go home for dinner. Our neighbors had an apple orchard and a white picket fence. We had a screened porch and a backyard set up for badminton, hula hoops, jump rope, croquet, or hopscotch. We rode bikes, ice skated on the Little Miami River, performed plays and songs with our cousins, sang hymns and Broadway hits at the piano with our grandmother, cut out paper dolls that mother bought us at the Five and Ten in Mariemont, and listened to 45 records like Rockin' Robin. We had handsome wardrobes for our Madame Alexander dolls and Barbie and Ken. We swung on vines out over the bluffs with the railroad trains below. The steam from the trains created a film over all the furniture in the house when the windows were open. My mother liked to listen to her records in the evening on the Hi-Fi.

We picked blackberries off the bushes and stained our little hands with our friend Linda Holmes. Jane Lambertson next door was a good pianist and played while we sang Sentimental Journey in harmony. We created harmonious sounds with water in crystal glasses while our mothers prayed we would not break them.

We ran as fast as we could down Pleasant Street; I was lightning fast and ran like the wind. A box was wheeled into the room one day, a black and white television, which had cartoons such as Popeye, Mighty Mouse, Howdy Doody: programs such as Mickey Mouse, Roy Rogers, Gene Autry, the Lone Ranger, Sky King and the renowned drama series, Hallmark Hall of Fame, all in black and white on a tiny screen.

Our sister Anne was born when we reached the age of seven, and we pushed her dutifully in her baby carriage. Another sister, Catherine, was born when we were ten. We saw them as babies and kept them safely in our room when our father, the Big Bad Wolf, came home from work. Our mother would call out, "Here comes your father," and we would scramble.

The younger sisters had their work cut out for them, coming from this cloth. At each school, the teachers queried, "Are you related to the Runyan twins?"

My paternal grandparents had purchased a farm in Batavia, Ohio, which they rented for alfalfa production. They lived in the house by the stream with very old-fashioned furniture. My grandmother was Ruth Van Pelt. Gammy told us stories about her father a Methodist preacher and the lynching of black men in Oxford, Ohio. She had been a schoolteacher and head of the Ohio Teachers' Association at one time. Herbert Runyan Poppy walked with a big crutch on his leg because of an auto accident and poor surgery in his youth; and he hid his pain well. He would walk with us down the lane to the big barn where the farmers dried their crops. Gammy ultimately joined the John Birch Society and could not tolerate the leftist or Communist movements. This aversion was no doubt furthered by the Communist scare in Washington, DC.

My father was an only child and played alone. He told me when Malinda died to remember that Tommy and Cubby were playing football on his bed spread, and Tommy had the football. I have now discharged that obligation which I never forgot.

One day when I was exceedingly small, I fell on the driveway and knocked out my front tooth. After the tragedy subsided, everyone was grateful that they could tell the twins apart because I was missing a front tooth.

Our family had unearthed genealogical miracles given my mother's interest and avid pursuit of family connections. Surrounded by intergenerational structures, our position in the white privileged class was assured. My mother traced both herself and my father's lineage back to the American Revolution and participated enthusiastically in the Daughters of the American Revolution which was powerful in Ohio. Beyond those credentials, we had at least three ancestors on the Mayflower, the boat which carried the Puritans away from religious persecution in England. The Wing family was prominent in her research, and my cut glass dish reads Wing Fort House, Sandwich, Massachusetts. Not satisfied with our credentials as yet, my mother discovered that family members attended the signing of the Magna Carta by the nobles of England in 1166. My mother assisted the Dames of the Magna Carta in southern Ohio. I feel no shame for this master status, only gratitude to our founding fathers.

My father's family settled the Ohio Territory and built numerous grand homes to celebrate their German heritage. Christian Waldschmit House, Pennsylvania House, all with little glass dishes to spark my memories, courtesy of my mother's travels to these museums.

For my mother, ancestry strengthened our position in society. She had no concept of intergenerational karma. It occurred to me later that the death of her two sisters from childhood illnesses and the lengthy illness of Aunt Sissy in childhood had isolated my mother. She was sent to Potsdam to stay with her grandmother while still incredibly young. She remembers the horse-drawn carriages and the oil lamps. She remembers always being alone.

Aunt Sissy (Mary Louise), my mother's only surviving sister, had married a surgeon, Calvin Skinner. They located to Central Avenue in Middletown, Ohio in a beautiful mansion with a swimming pool. My aunt painted pastel portraits for the steel magnates and their families. Five children were born, of whom three survived: my cousins Winky (Sarah Wing), Susu (Susannah Denise) and Margo Louise. We visited them often and swam like minnows in the cold spring water pool. The cousins rounded out the sign of the Pleiades, the seven sisters.

Mernie, our grandmother lived most of the time with Aunt when we were five Sissy. Lewis Hamilton had died of lung cancer in Middletown, and Mernie stayed on in the same bedroom where I remember him dying. She came to visit us in Mariemont several weekends each month. With her musical heritage, she often traveled down into Kentucky to collect crafts from Berea College and songs on 78 records from the hills and hollows. Jean Ritchie was her favorite. We adored these songs with her playing the piano and teaching us the lyrics. Our favorite was 'Old Daddy Fox', which I know by heart to this day.

Old Daddy Fox went out one night.
He prayed to the moon to give him light
For he had a long way to go that night before he came to his den O.

When he came to the farmer's yard
The ducks and the geese they thought it hard
That their sleep should be troubled and their dreams be marred
By the visit of Mr. Fox O.

Margery Runyan, PhD, LCSW

He grabbed the old gray goose by her neck
And quickly swung her over his back
Which made the old goose go 'quack, quack, quack'
And the blood came streaming down O.

Old Mother Slipper-Slopper jumped out of bed
And out of the window she popped her head
Crying 'John, John, the gray goose is gone,
And the fox is off to his den O.'

Old cousin John ran down the hill.
He blew a blast both loud and shrill.
Said Old Daddy Fox,
'That's sweet music, still
I'd rather be at my den O.'

When he came to his old den,
Out popped the little foxes, eight, nine, ten,
Crying, 'Old Daddy Fox, you'd better go again.
You had good luck to town O.'

Old Daddy Fox and his old wife,
They never had a better meal in all their life.
They ate without a fork or a knife,
And the young ones picked the bones O.

Source: Folk Song

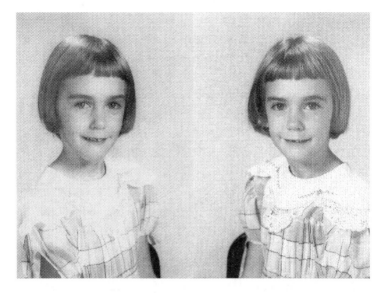

The Glorious Childhood

From infancy, Malinda and I were transported to our paternal grandparents' summer home on Lake Huron in Ontario, where we formed our primary identity as children of the natural world. This old clapboard cottage was built in 1903 by a confirmed bachelor who lived there hugging the lake with his housekeeper. My grandparents stumbled upon it in 1940 during one of their travels from Cincinnati, Ohio up through Detroit and into Ontario.

They gifted it to my father in 1945, perhaps for his marriage to my mother. My father was already in college at Ohio Wesleyan and went on to study at Cornell Law. He and his young wife, whom he had met at a luncheon counter in Cincinnati, loved the cottage with the view of the lake and the sounds of waves crashing in the lake's fitful moods. The lattice porch led out onto the sand beach where we played endlessly with our Indian villages, complete with tiny tipis from the nearby Saugeen reservation. Each year my mother drove us to the cottage in a 1957 Chevy station wagon that was green and white with little fins. All four girls sat in the back. In the early years, the roads were unpaved, and the drive took two days. I still remember the little cottages where we would stay overnight and the motel with a pool in Sarnia just across the border from Port Huron. As we traversed the

Ontario roadways, we would call out 'I see the lake.' Or 'how long before we get there?' On arrival, usually in the early evening, we would jump out of the car and run down to the water to greet our Great Lake once again.

Chantry Island was the dream world a few acres across from the beach.

The lighthouse is ingrained in my memory and the stories about the lighthouse keepers who endured the vicious storms were legendary. Our older friend David, who was the most creative of all of us, told us ghost stories about the lighthouse. Stories about trails of bloodstains across the log, footsteps heard coming up to the lighthouse peak, and winds that would moan and rail. David also was the director of the Cottage Capades, which the children performed every season for the adults in surrounding cottages. We would rehearse daily for weeks. Mostly we lip synced to popular records such as *Lipstick on Your Collar* and *Pink Cadillac*. Malinda and I performed a gypsy dance one summer with scarves that our mother supplied from fabric bolts.

David created other games for this swarthy crew of kids. He would wear a robe that my grandmother had brought to the cottage for sunbathing and take on the role of Master. We were his Slaves who had to do his bidding all day long. In the evenings, we would draw a large area for Capture the Flag on the beach. When it rained, we played board games in the cottages, particularly the side porch at our cottage where you could hear the waves crash and see the seagulls frozen aloft during the three-day blows. Other games were skipping stones, finding the prettiest stone, and jumping as far as we could off the swing set. We would mark where our feet landed for the farthest jump bragging rights. Once the free-swinging seat hit me in the head, and my mother took me to the doctor with a small hole from the seat edge.

We took tennis lessons at the Southampton Tennis Club right behind our cottage before we were tall enough to hold the racket. The teachers gave each child the opportunity to hit a forehand, a backhand, a net shot, a lob, and an overhead. Then we would rush around the court to pick up the balls and put them in the wire container. We played tennis as a family into my 50s, when I could no longer see the ball. My father won all the championships, and the tennis leaders named the final competition of the year after him.

In my memory, Malinda and I are huddled on the gray bedspread with strawberries in the South facing room. The eaves are still prominent and the night falls. She is launching a story with a single sentence, and we are alternating sentences to create the flow of events. This is a metaphor for the twin way. We can hear the tennis balls bouncing at the tennis club.

Another archetypal memory: Queen Anne's lace. The year that Queen Elizabeth toured the US to adoring crowds was the first time I heard that my mother looked like Queen Elizabeth. How synchronistic that my first wildflower love affair cathected on Queen Anne's Lace. To this day I am not sure who Queen Anne was, but the flowers were spectacular with their complexity and their lace like flower designs. They grew all along the road where we peddled our bikes.

Malinda and I rode our bikes on these same dirt roads to the end of the rainbow where we fully expected to find bags of gold or at least good fortune. Oddly, the rainbow would move as we got closer. We had to cross the Saugeen River to do this adventure, and so we must have been tweens by then.

These were my archetypes. The minnows that we used to watch at the edge of the lake, the big steady volcanic rocks towards which we swam and on which we perched to play king of the mountain. Red rock was the largest, most prominent, and most spotted with gray and black. Red rock proved perfect for King of the Mountain because there were many crevices to which one could cling. Black rock and yellow rock, otherwise known as flat rock, were harder to find when the lake was higher. We were always measuring our lives by the level of the Great Lakes and how far up the beach the lake came. Could we see it over the sand dune, or did we have to jump up see the lake?

One day we lost Anne. We found her way down the beach with some kind strangers almost at the long dock. Afterwards she had to wear a sign that read, "I am Anne Runyan and I live at Cottage 43." The cottages were numbered in the early days. Our cottage was smack dab in the middle of the Southampton beach, and you could see it clearly from the boats on the lake. All we had to do was just mention the big white cottage and people knew us.

Before the eaves were covered, bats used to come into the house through the open spaces. My mother's mother had covered these eaves to her chagrin because my fathers' parents wanted these spaces open. At least once per summer, we would huddle on the old wicker couch in the living room while my father took his trusted bat tennis racket upstairs to get the bats out of our bedrooms. Usually, a neighbor was recruited to help him. Our deepest fear was getting a bat talon stuck in our hair. It was the subject of waking nightmares.

The families from nearby cottages gathered at the beach for sunset each evening. The children ran on the beach, skipped stones, and executed cartwheels and somersaults. These same families had been associated for generations. Americans were few. The Robertsons who summered in the cottage behind ours lived in Cincinnati during the off-season. In the process of synchronicity, Uncle Robbie, Aunt Mary Louise and their four children shared a cottage with Aunt Mary Louise' sister Dorothy, settled in Ontario. Dorothy had two daughters who became our friends Meredith and Susan. Still another cousin living in Southampton to this day visits Annie and Al there. Many of the grown children returned to the seven hills of Cincinnati with its clustered neighborhoods, Hyde Park, Walnut Hills, Mount Adams, the Symphony, the Observatory, the Country Club. The downtown shop, Shillotos, is now a condominium. Annie and Al truly belong here in this place where, during all seasons, the extended childhood families from Southampton gather.

Our best friends in the cottage network were Ted Todd from Toronto and Harry Luscombe from Hamilton. Ted was paired with Malinda and Harry with me in our younger years. We literally did everything together. When they started in high school and taught tennis at the Club, we separated from them somewhat. Some summers we did not go to the cottage because we had jobs. I remember them flying on windsurfer sails to the horizon. I desperately wanted to be a young man who could fly. I wondered how far they would go before they turned back. My father would say, "Michigan is over there; start swimming."

After dinner we fed the seagulls with crusty day-old bread that Mother accumulated. She kept the slices in the breadbox above the refrigerator, and she would reach it down to us when it was time. We would run out on the beach with our friends and rip the bread into pieces. The seagulls would gather around us, with the babies on the ground with their gray coloring and the grownups in the air. Sometimes the adult seagulls would take the bread out of our hands or get so close that they would grab it out of the air. We would be surrounded by a large circle above and below on the beach. As we got older, we were introduced to Jonathan Livingston Seagull, a parable of the seagull who acted as Jesus to the other seagulls. He brought each bird to its own perfection. With the body dematerialized he had the ability to go anywhere, like the yogis in *Autobiography of a Yogi*. I still cry every time I think of this wonderful book which my grandmother manifested for us out of her extensive and deep love for books. Robert Moss suggests that we find the story we need for our life right now. Jonathan Livingston Seagull is the story I choose. Later when I learned to travel to the lower world as a shaman, the seagulls revealed that they as a species are one of my power animals.

My song:
Seagulls flying over the water,
Flying high in the sky so blue.
Seagulls flying over the water,
I wish that I were a seagull too.

Another power animal of mine is the fox. Annie reports their nesting under the deserted cottage in the spring and their escaping from civilization as the summer crowd invades. Another story of my life that I choose is *Le Petit Prince* (The Little Prince) by Antoine de Saint-Exupéry. A pilot flying mail across the Northern African desert into Algeria crashes and in his desperate state meets a little prince who has come from a tiny planet of his own with only one flower. Here on earth the little prince is overwhelmed by all the abundance and begins to wonder if his little planet is special. He meets a fox who asks to be tamed. Taming is creating ties according to the fox. 'If you come at four with a little treat, I will begin to be happy at three.

There must be rites.' The prince learns that the only things you embrace are the things you tame. 'The important thing is what cannot be seen.' The fox tells him that the prince has tamed his flower and so the flower is his. The prince bids the pilot adieu and returns to his home. The prince is the creative child who represents the dawn of a new life.

We can return to an old place physically while remembering a different life going forward from this place. I begin to imagine a life in Southampton as if it is another planet where I could have chosen to stay. Robert Moss creates a dream module entitled *Become a Conscious Traveler in the Many Worlds*. He believes there are many interactive worlds and parallel lives splitting all of time. In my study of dreams, Robert Moss became a mentor as I studied his courses on *The Shift Network*. I learned Active Dreaming, reminiscent of Jung's Active Imagination, and I discovered an elusive doorway. To my astonishment, I had a visit with Malinda while practicing contact with the departed.

Moss' instructions were clear: Choose from a variety of caves the one with the color that calls you forth. Enter the cave and emerge in a place where you will meet the departed ones. Dialogue with them if necessary and bring back a knowledge of the afterlife. My path led through a blue door shaped like a cave entrance, and I emerged on the shoreline of Lake Huron.

Malinda was waiting for me in her checked bathing suit with the white ribbon down the front. She smiled her shy smile and greeted me with no words. We got into a blue boat that was the exact boat that I now have in my carport in Florida: small motor, shallow hull, white bench seat, sixteen feet long. We were so confident heading out to Chantry Island off the Coast. We knew the Way. I jumped out of the boat and caressed Red Rock. As we left shore, she ran her hand over Black Rock where we spent many summer days sitting, diving, and climbing using the multiple hand holds.

We moored in a sheltered cove on the lee side of Chantry with crystal clear water exposing the rocks below. The harbor was shallow; we could see seashells, sand, coral, minnows; the water was radiant and clear. I realized why I loved the radiance. It is spiritual. The water was sparkling and rippling. We became seagulls. The radiance, the Divine White Light, the presence of the sacred, was blinding. The seagulls were flying overhead, and we transmigrated into birds, swooping and soaring. I remembered the story of Jonathan Livingston Seagull; he taught the other seagulls that they could time travel and space travel, change their shapes, live forever and help others.

Suddenly the afterlife revealed the deepest secrets; I would be free to soar, and all would be clear. The afterlife is sunny, warm, radiant, and beautiful. Seagulls are free. Malinda is one now. She will smooth out her angel wings in the white mansion on the hill (Block Island).

I time-traveled back to a movie theater that once upon a time flowered on the wide main street that led down to the dock and ancient lighthouse on Lake Huron. Somehow, we had money to pay the entrance fee. In the rows of seats, Malinda arrived achingly clear as a small child who evoked and mirrored my own small child with brunette bangs and sparkling, joyful blue eyes. She was I and I reflected mySelf in her. She did indeed live. I know that as a fact. She was both a dream and a constant presence.

Moss also taught us to recover those parts of our souls that had dissociated from the vital parts through trauma, anesthesia and life choices. At these crossroads we split into alternate paths in parallel universes. We must ask ourselves 'Where is the rest of me?' When we return to these old places, we can recover the lost parts of ourselves. If only I could recover the lost twin. Only fragments. I am at Red Rock in Lake Huron, the *prima matera* of my own alchemical journey. The Lake is high and Red Rock is submerged just as my unconscious is full of the lake-side memories. I so easily see her little legs and arms flailing and her crooked mischievous smile. It is as if she is myself. We are playing King of the Mountain on the rock surface. She is wearing the little checked bathing suit with the white ruffle; the same one she wore when she greeted me in the sacred dream. In truth, I did not differentiate my own appearance because I saw myself every day in Malinda. The rest of me is still there on Lake Huron. I cannot recover this lost part, but I can dream it.

I apprehended the ease of dream reentry. My dream soul went ahead of my body, respecting neither time nor space. I asked permission from the dream guardian who ensures that our intentions are pure. I clearly apprehend that the dreams were magical mirrors of my Self, and I set out to retrieve the lost pieces.

The universe became multi-dimensional. Alternate realities emerged. What if Malinda had not died? I found fresh words to entertain the spirits, embarked on shamanic journeys, and sought comfort in other planes of existence. The signs and symbols of everyday life revealed meaning; everything has been speaking all this time. Synchronicity created enchanted moments. The voices told me, 'Stories find you; make yourself available.'

The Animus and Anima

The Argonauts embark to recover the Golden Fleece and restore Jason to his proper right of kingship. They would have failed without the anima, the female force who counterbalances the male consciousness with her darkness and magic arts, the infamous Medea. Jason is the animus for Medea, her male counterpart, and Medea the unconscious force that provides the power, the life force, and the completion of the quest.

My father was brilliant and dark. When I was 16 or 17, my mother confided in me that she believed he was philandering. She had found lipsticks in his car, the VW Beetle, and he was developing different habits for washing the dishes. I was already deeply afraid of his rages, his solitude, his discomfort with the children. He ate a different meal after ours was finished, usually steak, asparagus and a martini. His arrivals aroused the terror of 'fe fi fo fum' as Jack stole the hen that laid the golden eggs. We hid in our rooms. Once he screamed at my mother, 'I will have you committed to an insane asylum,' and I believed he could do it. Or 'Why did you have these kids anyway? I never wanted them.' When I graduated from Goucher College in 1970, I came home to interview for jobs. I read *Lord of the Rings* late into the night. My father would rage at me to get out and find a job. Every day he raged and called the college to berate them for my ill preparation. The negative Animus ruled.

I had become a young woman who relied more on collective values and rational arguments than my own intentions and feelings, securing my parents' love through achievement and good behavior. I had a psychic fragmentation overlaid by a strongly marked persona of 'good.' Malinda was even more strongly marked by this need to comply with social norms. She listened to John, her husband, and complied with whatever he said, including getting on a plane in bad weather. Animus problems beget self-alienation.

The daughter must find her way to herself. Self-affirmation deprives the negative animus of its power. The endogenous libido derives from the kinship strengths finally devoted towards the growth of the self. The alternative is the *puella*, the life-long girl, who engages in endless flirtations with men and life.

My father did not go to World War II because he had rheumatic fever when he was a child. My sister Anne believes that he was less violent, less compelled towards manliness as a result. When the students were killed by the National Guard at Kent State University in 1970, in Ohio, where he had lived his life, he cried inconsolably. He had acted in Shakespeare at Ohio Wesleyan, and Anne described this behavior as more feminine than the average man in his cohort. He joined the Democratic party and supported George McGovern's bid for the presidency. He embraced the Palestinian cause and flirted with socialism as a doctrine. He was privileged with a brilliant Phi Beta Kappa mind and a law degree from Cornell, quite an elite accomplishment during the 1940s. My mother was also gifted with an Ivy League education at Smith College, and they encouraged us to become degreed and proficient in our fields.

Anne believes that her feminism arose from the times in the 1960s and 70s. She remembers that Malinda gave her a copy of the *Second Sex* by Simone de Beauvoir, *The Journals of Anais Nin*, books by Gertrude Stein and *The Alexandria Quartet* by Lawrence Dumas. These developments in her life arose out of the year that Malinda and I spent in Paris and Malinda's subsequent sojourn at home that next year. We all rode the currents of individual empowerment, whose persistence Anne ascribes to women of color in our current political climate. She supports the Global South movement in which women are seeking birth control rights and freedom from domestic violence. She teaches global politics and global feminism at the University of Cincinnati.

What a marvelous outgrowth of our family of all girls. A self-object is a person who strengthens one's personal self, increasing vitality and cohesion, supplying what is needed for wholeness. These self-objects affirm selfhood, perceptual reality, growth of self-esteem and regulation of intense affect. The sibling group of girls in our family conspired to grow the anima and to repress the animus that my father had poorly formed.

The quest for wholeness begins. The mandala represents the Totality of the Self, and the Self is the contents of the entire psyche. What falls outside this circle is noise. Inside me, what is closing? What is opening? There are four sacred worlds, four directions enclosed by Mother Earth and Father Sky, that must be honored in the four quadrants of the mandala. Using ancestors and spirit guides, I must create a ceremony to construct the mandala of my own life. The pendulum of my energy is swinging from Entropy (chaos) to Neg-entropy (order.) *The Secret of the Golden Flower*, Richard Wilhelm translator and CG Jung commentator, reveals a potent yellow center. By accident, my husband breaks a dish that Malinda gave me with a yellow center and black petals. The Taoist master that Bonnie and I found in NYC told Hank and me to put yellow in the center. My Taoist training places the yellow, the Earth, the Spleen, in the center. The circle is the format. This much I know. What goes into the circle becomes the question. Past, present, future.

The energy paradigm of the Self or mandala is the manifestation of the intent for wholeness. By intuiting that structure and the process within, we are given insight into the soul's evolution. How does this paradigm come into Being? How can we best 'see' it? How can we change it? Each Self has a unique energetic signature. The pattern appears as a mandala signifying wholeness. It encompasses all the aspects of the self, as fragmented and various as they may appear. Every situation draws forth or evokes the aspect of the self that is ready to absorb the lesson at any given space/time/point/event. The aspect meets the situation in a perfect way, in exactly the right way, to advance that situation to the next level of consciousness. This moment is then perfect in its wholeness and its resolution. The Anima is ready to advance as the heroine, thus rescuing the soul.

Rollo May has said, "Courage is ontological." I find the dialectic between conviction and doubt. I have no fear of death. I have no fear of taking the wrong path. I already accept that eating from the tree of the knowledge of good and evil is a fall upwards into consciousness. 'Do not go gentle into that good night.' Dylan Thomas would have us 'rage, rage! Against death.' Courage is the creativity to live beyond one's own death. I am required to express the vision within my own being using new symbols and new forms.

I begin to search within. What have been the benchmarks? Where have I found Truth thus far? Shall I look there again?

Theosophy

The School of Practical Philosophy on 79th St. East at the edge of Central Park in New York City provided a magnet for my curious mind. The advertisement in the New York Times offered a lived philosophy for the seekers of truth in everyday life, a way to transcend the materialism of modernity and the deep emptiness it has left. In Henry David Thoreau's book Walden, he states, *"To be a philosopher is not merely to have subtle thoughts, nor eve to found a school, but so to love wisdom as to live according to its dictates, a life of simplicity, independence, magnanimity, and trust. To solve some of the problems of life, not only theoretically, but practically."*

I studied at this school for approximately four years from 1980-85. I traveled into Manhattan through the Lincoln and Holland Tunnels, (depending upon my work site) racing uptown on Broadway and then dashing into the imposing brownstone just in time to slide into a seat before meditation began. The instructors were honored and served by the higher-level students, and the remainder had cleaning, cooking, and flower arranging duties for our service contribution. We studied Sanskrit letters, their pronunciation, and calligraphy.

After initiation into meditation, we learned that the head of the School was headquartered in London and owed the teachings to masters in the East. I also learned that the founders had gleaned Buddhist wisdom from India and translated it into terms palatable to Western traditions.

As my allegiance to the School grew, I lost track of the middle path (Tao) between my career and the School. I was supporting numerous programs for the New Jersey Department of Human Services, assigned to downtown Newark; developing social services was an unpredictable assignment that involved field work in five counties. The stress of arriving at School on time was unbearable, and eventually I surrendered to career demands. Still in my 30s, I had ambition and altruism to satisfy within a moral and ethical paradigm developed through social work education. The spiritual path was attractive but could not yet replace my worldly responsibilities.

Two decades later during an immersion in Buddhism at Tara Mandala retreat center in Pagosa Springs, Colorado, I returned to my questions about the School. Monastic Buddhism the Theravada as taught by the Buddha had made few inroads into Western life where householding predominates over quiet meditation and solitude. I wondered who had founded the school that had melded Buddhism into modernism. Where was the Tao, the path between? Could I find it now?

I began to wonder; when did I first encounter Madame Helena Blavatsky and her master works *Isis Unveiled* and *The Secret Doctrine?* I have no recollection of the term Theosophy from those early days at the School and yet my friend Sharon, whom I met at the School, was drawn to the same esoteric works. Looking back over my shoulder at the interior of the brownstone I can picture the library in the basement where powerful esoteric writings such as *Perennial Philosophy* by Aldous Huxley and tracts from Buddhism and Hinduism were sold. Is it possible that Mme. Blavatsky or at least her disciples were the founders of the School? Was the School linked back to the Tibetans she had visited in the late 1800s? She wrote in the Mahayana Buddhist tradition, espousing the Path of the Bodhisattva. Her writings were based on the *Stanzas of Dzygam* and *The Book of the Golden Precepts* (translated in *The Voice of the Silence* by Blavatsky) which are Buddhist, pre-Buddhist, ancient esoteric writings. She describes the reawakening of the Gods after a 'Night of the Universe' to the ultimate reunion of cosmos with divine source, thereby reestablishing Hermetic philosophy. *The Mahatma Letters,* written by Mme. Blavatsky's teachers, were also published in my lifetime. The teachers' aim was fostering a universal brotherhood based on altruism and manifesting the grand plan.

This esoteric tradition claims to be older than the Vedas. Its truths were embedded in ancient civilizations and codified in scriptures long buried.

The study of Hermetic philosophy is embodied in the *Kybalion*, published in 1912 and credited to three initiates who had studied the lost writings of Hermes Trismegistus in ancient Greece. They were known as Thoth in ancient Egypt. The seven laws of Kabbalism or magic became overt through this modern publication of ancient esoteric beliefs, and a segment of humanity began to understand this 'Truth' per Blavatsky.

1. Mentalism: The universe is all mind, the one mind of All. Father is knowledge, spirit, invisible. Mother is life and nature. Thoughts give rise to form. Spirit and nature combined equal Truth.

2. Vibration: Nothing rests; all is in motion.

3. Correspondence: As above, so below.

4. Polarity: Everything is dual; opposites are identical in nature and different in degree; all paradoxes may be resolved. Thesis and antithesis; extremes meet, good and bad are the same; mental alchemy can transform them.

5. Rhythm: Everything flows in and out, swinging like a pendulum, moving towards neutralization.

6. Cause and effect: Planes of causation obey laws, not chance, no coincidence. You can move to a higher plane to become a cause.

7. Gender is in everything for the purpose of regeneration.

Now I am wondering if a spiritual adviser 'as cause' recommended Alice Bailey, or if her writing just arose in the natural sequence of my journey. She is certainly a Theosophist and yet her numerous writings are not sold or even mentioned by the Theosophical Press. I began my inquiry with 'The Soul: A compilation.' This flowed into *Death, The Great Adventure* and eventually I gravitated towards *The Seven Rays* and *Esoteric Psychology.* Here is a philosophy garnered from the Tibetan (dare we say 'channeled' without accusations of Spirit-ism) that has a Platonist flavor of essential ideas being gradually brought to full fruition.

The Seven Rays are the energies that, from their emergence at creation, have shaped our personalities, our Souls and our undertakings as a human race. The Seven Rays are named: Will and Power, Love and Wisdom, Active Intelligence, Harmony through Conflict, Concrete Knowledge and Science, Idealism and Devotion, and Ceremonial Order and Magic. They wax and wane, overlap, and cooperate in the evolution of mankind. Each personality is infused with the energy of a ray for one lifetime as a lens or organizing principle, and the Soul ray persists throughout many lifetimes. The Soul ray endeavors to infuse the personality on the Path through various initiations. I believe that my soul ray is Love and Wisdom under the sign of Gemini and my personality ray is Harmony through Conflict under the sign of Taurus. I can still change my mind; this is not my choice but my calling.

Rudolf Steiner, theosophist, lights the path to higher worlds through the application of esoteric knowledge. The PATH is the way by which the human soul must pass in its evolution to full spiritual self-consciousness. No word of such knowledge will be imparted to anyone not qualified to receive it. One must adopt the attitude of 'the path of veneration,' of devotion to truth and knowledge. Materialism is a deterrent. We have the power to transform ourselves within the innermost self, beginning with the thought life. The Taoists also believe that our thoughts and intentions, the Yi, manifest in the Shen, Qi and Jing, and thus our actions. Provide for oneself moments of inner tranquility to learn to distinguish the essential from the non-essential.

We intuitively seek the Chita in Hinduism, 'Undisturbed by the unpleasant, longing no more for the pleasant, free from attachments, fear and anger is the steady state of the Chita.' Fear has no place. Within each lies the higher self which requires awakening, and so we begin to recognize that we belong to a higher world. The impressions of the outside world, the horizontal plane, must be managed and only allowed to influence the self as we choose. We meditate and discover that we strive towards a spiritual cosmic whole.

Certain persons have already passed through the initiation process as Fire Trial with a wealth of experience. They have born sorrow, disappointment and failure with courage and fortitude, equanimity and greatness of soul.

For these, knowledge of the higher worlds, spiritual learning and sight, and a devotion to duty prepare them to study the occult language necessary to reach the temple of higher wisdom. Gentleness, gratitude, and inner silence permit the soul to evolve inner tranquility. The organs coincide with energy points known as chakras, that open as petals on a lotus flower.

In this higher world, one is freed from the personal self and begins to see her inner self-reflected back to her as in a mirror. This reflection allows the owning of all projections of the shadow or demons as well as the visualization of the truths and virtues often personified as the five families or the hundred Buddhas of the initiation into Tibetan Buddhism.

Malinda has always been a reflection of my higher self. She evolved more rapidly and found an opportunity to leave samsara behind and achieve Buddhahood. Many Buddhas then return as Bodhisattvas to alleviate suffering on earth as she may have chosen. On the mountain where she lay dying her husband did not realize the prayers within the *Book of Natural Liberation from the Betweens*. In the 49 days of Bardo she still was granted the chance to gravitate towards the clear light and may have attained Buddhahood. If so, I can visualize her as a Buddha, a Dakini or a Tara but which one? In the Vajrayana tradition I can absorb her, the jewel ruby and the sound syllable, into my heart. She is, however, already lodged there.

The twin is the inner other, the immortal self, the one who goes through life at our side, the magical traveling companion, compensatory in all respects. Just as Jung believed that the unconscious compensates for imbalances in the consciousness, so we shared the personal unconscious through experience, the collective unconscious through genetics, and two conscious minds that we bended into one set of thoughts. We were mirrors for each other. We finished each other's sentences and shared a single thought process. Telepathy was the least of our paranormal abilities. We formed worlds and dissolved worlds in our amplified imaginations. Our sensory input was vast, stimulating, beautiful, full of wonder because we knew ourselves as one whole and thus powerful beyond our wildest dreams. The gods and goddesses of the world myths often possess Twinship because it bestows a miraculous nature.

I encountered Theosophy again in the organization IONS, which is also seeking the intersections between religion and science. Scientists have proven that Consciousness is universal, infinite, all-encompassing. Is materialism facing extinction? Why do so many of us worship modernism, technology and even the scientific method? Do the senses rule, or are there worlds beyond our limitations? I am committed through my studies, my writings and my psychotherapy practice to assist in the unfolding of the Age of Aquarius and humanity's return to spiritual enlightenment.

The Landmark Forum

One day in 1998, a kind and intelligent administrator in the NJ Department of Human Services invited me to go to an event with her that proved to be an introduction to the Landmark Education series. This program, a successor to EST founded by Werner Braun and purchased by the facilitators when he fell from grace, entitled the Landmark Forum, was a large group weekend experience which changed my life once again.

I learned powerful distinctions that allowed me to disconnect my mind from the endless chatter of poor me and engage with the future more meaningfully. Modeled on Phenomenology per Husserl and the philosophy of Heidegger, we learned to take responsibility for our projections and live more powerfully into the future. I might well have remained with this program throughout my life and become a trainer; so many people were being served to attain another level of maturation. The forums covered Leadership and Self Expression; Communication, Power and Performance; the Advanced Forum; required service and took perhaps two years to complete. This path was very straight and filled with light.

Our assignments were empowering:

1. Do something totally outrageous for yourself.

2. Acknowledge one person per day for no reason so that they are totally known and appreciated.

3. Clean an area that has been a mess.

4. Have a miracle happen.

5. Call someone you have not talked to in six months.

6. Perform an extraordinary act of kindness.

7. Do something for yourself that you should be doing.

8. Make a difference for one person without them knowing it is you.

During the Advanced Forum, the trainer provided a metaphor of being in a plane that is plummeting downward, and we are unaware that it will soon crash. He exhorted us to create powerfully in these moments before the unknown future arrives. I was completely astounded that he described the exact experience of Malinda's death. I was so excited to tell him that I had lived this. The line that stretching to him seemed endless. I found myself outside, trying courageously to draw breath here on Earth and looking into the stars where I found inspiration. I imagined that Malinda was one of the stars, one of the saints in the firmament of heaven, and that she was looking down on me asking me to love. I had unconsciously decided that I would never love on earth the way I had loved her. I was simply awaiting my death to rejoin her. In that moment, a ray of hope pierced my heart and brought a simple decision that I would love again, perhaps not exactly, but grandly and generously. My heart opened like a flower of love. I greeted the revelation with a commitment to love and serve for as long as I was here on earth.

In the Landmark Forum, I learned about the Winning Formula. This formula is compulsive behaviors that we engage throughout our lives instead of accepting that human life is essentially empty and meaningless. The paradigm is built during our youth and young adulthood during three critical periods: toddlerhood, adolescence and early to mid-20s. The incidents are terrifying moments of annihilation that we are not clear that we can survive. In the moment, we adopt identifications that allow us not only to survive that event, but also to never have such an event again, if possible. We are defended and protected by these identities. Mine are Free Spirit, Loyal Friend, and Smart One.

Free Spirit: The first component for myself was hitting Malinda with a pail on the beach in Southampton when I became the bad twin and then the Free Spirit, never again dependent upon my mother's positive regard. We were three or four years old, and I remember my mother's horror to this day. I flew away and claimed my freedom from her judgment.

Loyal Friend: The second component arrived in my teen years when I followed the Bad Boys down into the woods and drank beer with them. Perhaps I even kissed one of the boys. The next day all the girls in my crowd knew about this transgression and decided to ostracize me. They called me from Gale Griese's house to notify me of my outsider status and to vilify me; I was mortified. School became torture. I identified with the Bad Girl, the Bad Twin, the Evil Twin, who should be ashamed of herself. Was Malinda part of the cabal? Most likely she was. She was compliant and I was rebellious. At this moment, I decided to become a Loyal Friend and never ostracize a human being. I stuck to this position firmly throughout my life, advocating for the weak, the isolated, and the lonely, in both my career and personal life. Only in my 50s did I begin to let go of friends in order to flow with my life. Before then, once my friend you were always my friend.

The Smart One: The final component occurred during my VISTA Volunteer year when I lived on 39th and Chestnut Street in Philadelphia and volunteered with the Reverend Leon Sullivan in his organization, OIC (Opportunity Industrialization Corporation). My program was Adult Education, which took us down into the ghettos to meet with neighborhood groups on their blocks and train on exercising legal rights, getting power with City Hall, and developing writing skills. The recruiters would go on the block to find a leader willing to hold the meetings and others interested in attending. My part was educating on getting blocks cleaned, removing abandoned cars, beautifying neighborhoods, and basically giving information about how to get all this done. One night I made the critical mistake of using the term 'boys' to refer to the youth in the meeting. No one wanted to talk to me at the office for the next few weeks. I remember walking into the luncheonette and the recruiters pointing at me. I decided, 'never mind.' I am smarter than they are, so I will just work at something where brains count. At that moment I realized that Malinda died at 39 and I lived at 39th and Chestnut.

Synchronicity has always been there.

The capstone of my legacy from Landmark was given to me while I was serving as a helper in an advanced class. I was honored to be chosen to write calligraphy on the blackboard, pass out papers, and help the students in every way. The reading that I learned goes as follows:

Standing in a clearing for unforeseen and unimaginable futures to occur, begin to create a future for your life - a future that could transform the actual content of your life to that which is unforeseeable. A future that only occurs in the moment it is said to be. Futures are not the past undistinguished as such. The future exists in the integrity of the listening. Am I willing to establish integrity for that future to be fulfilled?

Assignments related to speaking myself into the future I created:

1. Call the person who has accepted to be the integrity of listening and speaking the future

2. Complete with one person from the future you have constituted yourself to be.

3. Contact two people in your community and share the future that you are.

4. Acknowledge someone in your family each day from your future.

5. Share with someone what is happening in your life out of constituting yourself as a future

6. Watch for breakthroughs and miracles.

Ultimately, I spoke myself into existence as the Possibility of Peace and Joy.

The rest of my life has manifested that future with integrity. My psychotherapy practice, my relationships with extraordinary people, the hope I have instilled, the meditations I have learned and transmitted are all manifestations of Peace and Joy.

From that point forward, my life experience has multiplied. Clearly there are alternative realities, and I can live in them all. Time is a curvature of space, and clock time 'tick tock' is a social contract. There is plenty of time and time is my friend. I created two homes in two different settings and fell in love with both energies, the ocean and the mountains. Two businesses, two offices, two cars, two communities, two sets of clients, two ways of seeing the world in two universes.

The Ascension

The Ascension can be mythologized as the ascension of Jesus from the tomb. Later seen by his disciples, he is transfigured and only visible to the ones ready to see him. These are the initiates who with human eyes are able to see spiritual truths.

Castor and Pollux, the twins, are brothers to Clytemnestra and Helen, Greek princesses who figure prominently in the Trojan War. They also ascend to the heavens as stars in the firmament.

With hope as my companion, I determined to find my Higher Self through spiritual study and practice. Finally, my strength began to return and with it the capability to explore higher realms where I had never dared go. I felt worthy to delve into the wisdom of prophets who had surely been sent to enlighten us. Carl Gustav Jung was an obvious choice. I began to read *The Red Book* and collect his published works. Although warned by my Jung mentor that this work was unreadable, I pressed forward with deep understanding and gratitude. When I discovered the Symbolic Life per Jung, I knew then how to live. This path has changed my worldview to observe and conceptualize at a deeper level. All events are symbolic; all words are sacred; all actions are ceremonial.

Hinduism was always on my radar from the days when the great gurus were transported to the United States from India to teach in our venues. I had met them in New York City and pursued a robust yoga practice. I committed to reading the Vedic works that were accessible.

The crucial piece in my puzzle was Buddhism. I attended the Tara Mandala retreat center and began to read the Sutras. I opened my heart to the virtues espoused by the Buddha and practiced 'Feeding Your Demons' in psychotherapy. I learned and integrated the meditation in my clinical practice and my life. If anyone could ascend to these heights, I had certainly paid my dues through suffering. Years in samsara clinging to the past had prepared me to let go.

At this time, I had progressed deeply through the First Initiation as the Theosophists describe it. I had consciousness of the Monad or the Soul and could see the Path more clearly, the journey towards the evolution of all that is within the Grand Plan. As a whole humanity is still progressing through the First Initiation per Alice Bailey, I had no intention of waiting for the Others.

I was exhausted by the paths that metaphysics provided. I had explored the ontological questions of What is there? Who Am I? I had asked the hard epistemological questions such as What constitutes reality? Is it only materialism? Are there only sensory modes of knowing? And I had come to grips with the essential truths of Right/Wrong, True/False and the existence of Beauty. I knew that matter is a projection of consciousness and that we are Gods.

Philosophy had presented the questions of the nature of knowledge, the bases for conduct, and the best forms of governance given our nature as humans. Socrates (469 - 399 BC) made his choice of death by hemlock rather than relinquishing the Truth that the unexamined life is not worth living. So, did I know this already? What had I contributed to make my survival and Malinda's death worth something?

Plato had given me a strong sense of past and future, life before birth and life after death. He believed in the transmigration of souls, that the soma or body is the prison of the soul on earth, that the soul is liberated at death so it can reclaim its truths. Knowledge on earth in a physical body is clouded by the senses. Truth predates human experience and can be reclaimed through reminiscence of previous lives. Had I lived all my life thus far in Plato's cave? Had I failed to turn around the see the Truth in the light of day?

I was ready to find the Truth in the great world religions. But first, I had to encounter my Unconscious.

*****

The Jungian Analyst

Progressively feeding myself with higher frequencies, I awoke to find myself in the embrace of Carl Gustav Jung, the brilliant Swiss psychiatrist who founded analytic psychology. The *Conjunctio*, the alchemical union of East and West, enlightened my energy body once again. The Tao of the symbolic life became my truest passion. Per Jung, for the first half of our life we circumambulate the ego; for the second half the ego relents, and we circumambulate the soul. For the first half, we learn lies through family, community and peer groups in the process of being socialized into societal norms. In the second half, we learn to undo all that and find our own belief system about ourselves, our journey, our highest purposes.

Embarking on a psychotherapy practice in 2008, I committed to a holistic approach with a focus on Carl Gustav Jung because he seemed most capable of crossing the immense divide between East and West. His approach to the unconscious also coincided with my many experiences of archetypes that appeared to me to be collective. The archetype of Two. The archetype of Twins. I shared these numinous vital energies with Malinda, so we must have been destined in some way to live in that world populated by twos and twins. Synchronicity also convinced me that there is a vast web of reality outside of our perceptual field that produces simultaneous, related events without apparent causation. I began to realize and to truly accept that alternate realities exist on many planes of existence, including lives that we did not choose to experience.

In Jungian theory we have an inner other, a twin, our immortal self who goes through life at our side, a magical traveling companion whose interventions are compensatory. Would that mean that Malinda had stayed with me as a spiritual guide? The Tao teaches that sages and masters use microcosmic

111

orbit and other practices to create spiritual bodies, available in the moment of death that they can occupy. Could it be that Malinda went ahead to occupy the spiritual body that we had created from the Twinship and that she was living nearby on another plane?

I became deeply committed to helping my clients achieve wholeness, wherever they found themselves on the journey of life, the path that leads forward and upward. I grasped the meaning of the Beatles 'Long and Winding Road' that leads to your door will never disappear; I've seen that road before. Don't leave me standing here; lead me to your door.' I knew we were all headed back to the Light, the Source, the Godhead, and many people had lost track of themSelves. For Jung, the Self is the wise master.

Per the *Bhagavad Gita* and the *Upanishads*, the Self is whole, pure, wise, indivisible, unknowable. It is the Oneness of All.

The four primary aspects of Jungian psychotherapy:

1. The interpretation of dreams in order to amplify the archetypes in the collective unconscious that need to be symbolized in this person's life.

2. The process of individuation which is the journey towards the fullest actualization of the Self.

3. Active imagination for the full exploration of the Self.

4. The analytic encounter with the Self's transference and countertransference within the closed beaker of the relationship.

The process of individuation begins with the 'participation mystique' a state of identity with the 'object' such as the family, the religion and the culture. The developing ego experiences optimism, physical growth, ideas, emotions, desires and the assertion of the will. At 18-21 we emerge from a cloud and see who we are/are not, what we want/do not want, and come to the center of ourselves. The ego emerges out of the unconscious in clouds of glory, and we begin to separate from the collective. At 35-40, we have a dawning sense that life is not eternal. We face the awareness of death, first perhaps for our parents, and later our cohort. We are asking, 'Do I want to live my life this way?' 'Is there a higher meaning?' 'How can I achieve my maximum potential?'

Eric Noeman, an Israeli disciple of Jung, believed that there are three stages of individuation. The matriarchal where we experience nurturing, safety, protection, dependency and few demands for performance. In 6th or 7th grade the expectations of society increase, and we enter the patriarchal stage where responsibility, duty, consequences, performance, authority, judgment and structure take hold. The ego must cope and adapt. Ultimately the individual separates from the patriarchy and takes a narrower road towards wisdom. We must free ourselves from cultural constraints in order to find the Essential Self. Modernity, utilitarianism, technology and science become devoid of meaning and we must step outside of modernity to search for the Soul. This era is characterized by individual decisions, non-conformity, self-awareness, reflection, introspection, synchronicity, and a fuller synthesis of the Self. We open the door to dreams, active imagination and divination such as the I Ching and the Tarot in order to consult with the Self. We seek the joining of the opposites to achieve the transcendent function.

In his *Red Book* where Jung confronts his own unconscious, Jung describes some of his methods of treatment that are based on exploring fantasies. He believed that the exploration of fantasies from the personal and impersonal sphere is a process of initiation. Consciousness participates and a purposiveness develops out of the recesses of the deep. These goals are:

1. The assimilation of the personal unconscious.

2. The differentiation of the persona from the core of the self.

3. Overcoming the state of god-likeness.

4. Integration of the animus or the male aspect of the self.

5. Inner dialogue with the animus. The animus is seeking the father and other men who arouse the feelings of the patient.

Jung's experience of the inner male companion is Philemon, the old man who welcomed the gods into his home in Ovid's *Metamorphoses* and became sacred. He and his wife Baucis died at the same moment. Jung considered him to represent superior insight and often consulted him on important matters while walking in his garden.

For Jung, modern suffering is related to the waning power of religious symbolism to heal psychological fragmentation. The goal is the Center through the circumambulation of the Self in the symbol of the mandala, the realization of the wholeness of the Self. This higher identity follows the death of a lower identity. The old identities are relinquished for the new identification with the Whole. The Self comprises the full scope of a personality from individual traits to generic attitudes and experiences, actual and potential. It is the archetype of Wholeness.

The problem for twins in becoming and staying whole is the parental projection. We face the darker side as we begin to recognize the shadow within. The parent will project the bad twin on one and the good twin on the other. This defense against their own splitting causes splitting in the twins.

The one twin tries so hard to be good that she represses her shadow side. The other twin eventually gives up on pleasing the parents and explores her shadow. This twin has the better chance of taking responsibility for all beings in an existential and Buddhist sense. Once the parents have erected the Berlin Wall, or the Great Wall of China, or perhaps Trump's Border Wall, duality begins, and duality leads inevitably to conflict and repression of the shadow. It also generates paranoia that The Other is hostile and thus we blame The Other rather than accepting our part and becoming whole.

The treatment for the good twin is to recognize her shadow and not project it on the parents or the other twin. The treatment for the bad twin is to allow her to embrace wholeness, to love the shadow, and to celebrate her strengths. She is the one who got away and has the easiest path to individuation. Both must acknowledge the heroic journey. Both must follow her own myth, accept the burden of her life, experience suffering, find wisdom and allow intuition to flower.

The projection of evil is manifested in symbols and archetypes in all cultures. The fairy tales provide the Wicked Witch and the Evil Stepmother; Greek mythology and Jewish religion provide the Scapegoat and the healing ritual of harmony restored in the community once the evil one has left. The scapegoat archetype is the strongest one; she will carry all the painful emotions and so-called sins within her so that the common good and sense of community can be restored. Of course, King Lear and Oedipus the King come to mind immediately. Also, the Sacrificial Lamb is evoked.

Other projections of evil include vampires, hungry ghosts, darkness, chaos and sin. People all over the world are accepting these projections because their boundaries are weak and thus susceptible to the intrusion of toxicity. Some will never recover from the projection and die in despair or even suicide. These negative complexes can live in the energy body, consume the Qi, attack the physical body, cause disease, and kill. We locate them in psychotherapy so that they can be arrested in their development and dissipated. This dissolution can occur through Medical Qigong, Shen Gong, Feeding your Demons practice from Buddhism, hypnosis and age regression, and cognitive reorganization. The client says to herself "I am the victim of bad luck, bad circumstances, bad people." We can uncover this repetitious thinking and empower the client to think of herself as the co-creator of her own world.

Which twin will take the burden? The parental projection is very powerful and will entrap the unwary infant. Perhaps she is not eating properly or throwing up more. Perhaps she cries more. The mother may hand her over to another significant other to soothe. Perhaps the father has compassion for the little one and holds her more. Perhaps they are taught to let the children cry because Benjamin Spock says so. The die is cast.

In Montreal, at the conference of the International Association of Dreams, the window of my hotel room overlooked the mountain where Malinda died. My friend Robert Van de Castle, now deceased, wrapped me into the arms of the association, introducing me to the powerful dream theorists and researchers, implying that we would be a couple. My dissertation on the dreams of twins relied totally on Dr. Van de Castle's earlier studies of the content in dreams. He and Calvin Hall developed a control group and designed a coding system for quantitative dream interpretation. Dr. Van de Castle died several years after assisting me with my dissertation.

The dance and costume party figured centrally, and I had mirrors covering my outfit. At the speaking part, I shared, 'I dreamed I had a twin and when I awoke, she was gone.' Was she a dream figure? Was she a symbol of my higher self whom I had glimpsed during spiritual practice? The mirror neurons that enabled our symmetry cried out for her physical presence, while my evolving self knew that I had to transcend physicality and enter the world of symbolism.

Surviving Victimhood

This retreat into dreams and fantasy provided the touchstone for my dissertation, "Do Twins Dream Twin Dreams?" and the opportunity to arise from the old self into a rebirth of a higher self. The old worldview had fixated me as a victim, and through the convergent processing of dreams with waking life, my psyche formed a new synthesis from the bifurcation of old and new, of Malinda's life and death.

I learned this evolutionary process and function of dreams from Rossi. The old self had borrowed her worldview from my anxious controlling mother archetype. In dreams this viewpoint was loosened. Family figures grew and changed, evolving after death into compassionate helpers.

Dream: I was working towards a certificate and the exam was incomprehensible. Two girls already had copies and were assisting each other. These teacher's pets were given special favors. I got another copy, and my calm loving father offered to help me.

Comment: Thus, my mother (the teacher) and my sisters (her pets) achieved their goals of closing the family system by ostracizing and denigrating my father and me. My father had become my ally in dreams. No doubt such dreams reflected my mother's rejection of the bad twin or the wrong twin and her relief at my father's death; she had escaped from his tyranny and his undiagnosed mental illness.

My father changes into an animus figure in my dream worlds, smart, loving and helpful. He becomes the Philemon from Jung's garden stroll, the inner male companion.

Dream: I was teaching Community Organization in a huge room. Which end of the room to use? Downstairs behind the door the students could not hear me. I asked them to come upstairs. More arrived in carts from other classes and I was expecting a hundred in total. I went outside the front door and hostile horrible animals were attacking me. I was flailing and kicking and could not reach the door. Suddenly they disappeared.'

Comment: The demons are the unconscious material arising. The teaching is the mental body or consciousness making sense out of the new, forming a new world view. Organizing the material to share with the community as a gift. I am envisioning my return from the hero's journey after encountering the demons in the dark underworld. I am affirming resurrection and rebirth. Crisis is the antechamber, the testing on the path of purification. In the dreams, I am passing through the period of the Burning Ground or the rebirth prior to the first spiritual initiation.

This awakening of the Godhead within the heart accompanies the introduction to white magic, great changes in attitude and interpretation of life events, greater sensitivity to love, the seeking of the spiritual path, and encountering the soul. The seventh ray energies of the sacral creative center are sublimated into the throat chakra to unleash a burst of creative energy. In Jungian terms, the transcendent function arises through the dialectic tension of the conscious and unconscious meeting. The Imagination is unleashed to create new worlds, new myths, new symbols, an expansion in which time and space are no longer relevant.

Paul Brutsche also describes this process of unfolding through the stages of growth into the symbolic life – the ability to open the meaningfulness and power of the symbolic life in dreams and through the unconscious. I recognize this process, the emotional catharsis of tragedy and trauma; the structuring through compression and concentration of a well-ordered cosmos; the consciousness of shadow aspects of the origins; reactivation of childhood reconnection with archaic origins and ultimately the symbolization through the transcendent functions into a new vision of one consciousness, that is open, silent and free. Dreams open the door to this new world. What are the rules in this place? I diligently sought a formula in dreams, in philosophy, in ancestry, in science, in esoteric literature.

The Journey within the Self

The primary journey here takes place within the Self. There are locked doors and dark rooms. One thinks of the protagonist in Ingmar Bergman's film *Through a Glass Darkly,* who is ultimately hospitalized because of the inner God complex of a huge spider trying to have sex with her. These doors that create so much denial, so much avoidance, so much repression can be opened in the safe space of the psychotherapy. The psychotherapist can accompany the suffering client on an inward journey to recover these lost parts of the soul. Perhaps this is shamanism. If so, be prepared to go.

Celebrate your powers to make the parts a whole. Help to build the transcendent function and unify the split. For Jung it was his tower at Bollingham. Each client finds her way to reunite the bad and good projections and work her way up Jacob's Ladder, step by step. This occurs gradually in most and in the form of spiritual awakening in others. For some people, great projects are completed. The Bean Stalk is another climb, this time through magic and magicians who make the irrational understandable and restore us to prosperity via the Golden Goose.

Jung posits six levels of consciousness, discovered in every individual, consistent in human development. The first is the participation mystique where all is whole, all of nature is part of us, and we are part of nature. There is no separation between individuals and objects. Power objects such as stones carry magic, a type of animism enabled through projective identification. This is the Neptune stage of living in the womb surrounded by resources. Of course, the twin is already stressed into a duality where she must struggle for space, food, and survival. Will she have to absorb the other twin to get enough nutrition? Can they find a way to survive together? This is an important decision. The stories of phantom twins and so-called Siamese Twins rebound in the literature. Sometimes one twin chooses not to live until birth, and her soul takes another path.

The second level of human consciousness creates a distinction between physical objects and spiritual powers such as appear in classical myth. The spiritual world has its own autonomy in a metaphysical realm. The third is judgment of spirits, the expulsion from the Garden of Eden creates a dualism of good and bad and an eternal struggle between Jehovah and the evil spirits. The fourth is science, empiricism and rational thought, denial of the metaphysical. The fifth is spirits as reality, honoring the unconscious and archetypes, complexes and autonomous psychic forces. The sixth and final level is the *unus mundi*, the one world, with the archetypes rooted in the cosmos and the world anchored in synchronicity. Here reality is a composite of destruction and construction. Mankind must traverse these stages to reach the wisdom of interconnectedness.

And now in rereading *The Great Ideas of Philosophy*, lectures by David Robinson PhD in the *Great Teaching Courses* on Audible, I am impelled to consider the nature of causation within Empiricism. Plato believed in Innate Ideas underlying the ephemeral sensory input. By the 17th century, John Locke and then David Hume had adopted a materialist and naturalist perspective that the sum of man is his sensory experience. Hume went so far as to say that causation is a distorted mental model based on repetition, correspondence or sequence rather than a proven scientific principle per Frances Bacon and Isaac Newton. We now know from quantum mechanics (physics) that there is no linear causation; all systems are interrelated.

I was trained that Jung was an empiricist at heart; you are the sum of all your experiences. Jung's genius, in its proximity to psychosis, encountered the Idea as Essence. He theorized the existence of the Archetype glowing in the collective unconscious and the Symbol which reveals it. Jung's method for engaging clients in symbol formation using active imagination paralleled his own struggles in the *Red Book*. I believed that his fantasies from the personal sphere are his process of initiation, that consciousness participates, and that purposiveness develops.

Images are unconscious fantasy activity, inner reality that outweighs external reality. We see this condensed expression of the whole as the greater psyche. An archaic image is based on mythology. It is the precursor of an Idea. If an image is charged with numinosity, with psychic energy, then it becomes dynamic and will produce consequences. The image is the instinct's perception of itself. As we find with the Tao, whoever speaks in primordial images, speaks with a thousand voices.

Archetypes are preexistent, archaic, and universal energies in the collective unconscious; they are the charged particles of humanness. The constellation of an archetype leads to a relativization of time and space, and one can experience synchronicity and alternate realities. The sixty-four hexagrams of the *I Ching*, the Taoist system of divination, are examples of archetypes mirrored as situations in life. Given the complexity of life, there is an alarming poverty of symbols to elucidate the infinity of archetypes. Acausal order presents itself out of the logos as synchronicity, a constellation of archetypes that births relativity. It is characterized by an experience of parallelism, subliminal perceptions, forgotten memory, and inexplicable knowledge.

Symbols become numinous constellations which lead the conscious mind into a deeper synthesis of consciousness. They are the core of any complex; they synthesize opposites and manifest in time and space. They point the way to an archetype. They are nuclear material, powerful psychic energy whose meaning needs to be revealed through a connection to the depths of the unconscious. Symbols provide a bridge between the unconscious and the consciousness. A symbol can repeat itself and repeat until one is able to grasp it. Symbols are non-discursive, have multiple meanings, and are not specific. As such, they are like notes in music or art. Once the meaning is known within a particular context, the symbol becomes a 'sign' that stands for some other object as a substitution. Signs belonging to the conscious mind manifest as symbols to the unconscious. They become a precise language when invested with projective identification.

Jung immersed himself in the study of alchemy in the latter part of his life. Through his wife's wealth, the family was able to acquire numerous ancient texts that most scholars found impenetrable. Many other alchemical texts have been lost or destroyed in the Fire of Alexandria. Jung believed that the alchemists were engaged in spiritual transformation through the metaphor of material experiments. His knowledge of ancient languages allowed him to decipher the surviving texts from antiquity.

The alchemical process has four primary stages: the *Nigredo*, the *Albedo*, the *Rubedo* and the *Citrinitas*. The *Nigredo* is the black cloud of chaos taken to mean the state of the destructive aspect of the unconscious, including depression, primitive drives and dissociating factors. In the albedo, washing purifies the Prima Materia into whiteness. The *Rubedo* adds the element of red between white and black, fleshing out the continuum of consciousness. Lastly, the *Citrinitas* arrives where we find the green and yellow, or the wholeness of the psyche. This is the dawn of the new Self, unique in all the world, founded on the stone of the Prima Materia and yet able to flow with the tides of life and manifest what is right for its own journey.

The *Identificatio* is psychological conformity with objects. *Separatio* is when the naive projections by which we have molded the outside world and our own character are withdrawn. We transcend the *Conjunctio*, or the union of opposites, into growing the Self. A new wholeness of the godhead, awareness that the duality is still there but focused on the spiritual ascension to the highest concentration of light. The initiate pays the price of suffering to achieve the Oneness with the Self which is indestructible. Is this the gold of the alchemists, this transcendence of space and time, owning one's own projections, and climbing the mountain to the highest realms of the upper world? Here we meet guides in many forms who inform us as to the next level of self-growth.

I made the decision to strengthen my ego in order to survive through incomprehensible events and to forge a destiny that endures the truth and withstands the currents of life and time. This continuity of self would study dreams, myths, archetypes and philosophy as a preparation for death and the afterlife. I determined to release the grip of the personal and collective unconscious to compensate for the loss of myself and show me the path to the underworld. There Poseidon, Persephone, Osiris would meet me and release my shadow. I would manifest the courage to walk in darkness, connect with the souls who had passed through the veil, and hear the voices of the ancestral spirits.

Elizabeth Anne Hill (Twin Souls) lost her identical twin in a vehicle accident and sensed her passing over. In her view, the veil is a forgetfulness that covers the truth of our essential spiritual nature and our ultimate return to Source. I decided to remember as the worshipers are encouraged to do during the Eucharist when the priest intones: "Take and eat. Do this for the remembrance of me." The Eucharist is the remembrance and embodiment of souls whose bodies may have died but whose spirit still lives in us. I knew without knowing that if I lower my frequencies just slightly and increase my vibration, Malinda and I can sense, hear and feel each other.

I knew from Jung's change of course around 1912 that the libido within the unconscious can be transformed through symbolism and provide a teleological orientation that would provide the strength to live forward, not backward. I did not have to sublimate the despair and the rage. My remaining life on earth could not be determined by past events. I could transform the pain within me into the primordial energy of the life force, which I later knew as Qi according to the Tao.

The transcendent function is the doorway that allows the Unconscious to manifest. Dreams, myth and symbols are the vehicles that carry archetypal material into the middle world where souls meet with nature on earth. I spoke the words "I am what I lived, and I have had everything that I lived, and that is everything." Humankind is a doorway through which consciousness passes to illuminate the creation. The world is a product of that Consciousness which is everything and everywhere. The self, the whole range of psychic phenomena, as the Sanskrit reveals in the Gita, is whole, pure, wise, all knowing, far shining, assigning to every period its proper duty.

In order to individuate as the full potential of myself and the Self, I must descend into the shadow of the personal, collective, societal and cultural unconscious. I must uncover the divine white light and free the life force within. This I would do for the love of twins. Through the alchemy, I would achieve wholeness; the mandala of myself would become larger and brighter in order to contact the animus mundi, the soul of the world. I had the potential to redeem and resurrect myself.

Only then could I go to the star which is my own and Malinda's. The constellation of stars at our death is imprinted and recurs at our rebirth. I just did not understand if Malinda would resurrect in my same soul family from the same star.

Hinduism

Like Allen Shaw in *Twin*, I searched tirelessly for the piece of my soul that would make me whole again. I manifested belief systems in my 20s that gave me solace. They appeared to me at different stages in my development through the agency of inspired companions. Ingrid Stone who founded God's Love We Deliver, the home delivered meals for AIDS patients in New York City, had been my yoga teacher. She introduced me to Hinduism, and I followed Muktananda as my guru for several years. Friends and I traveled to meet him at a retreat center just north of the City. We sat patiently chanting Om Namah Shivaya until our turn came to present our gifts of fruit and flowers. The long procession down into the center of the mandala was a succulent taste of Siddha Yoga, and I was transported to a higher frequency as I neared the Holy One. The term 'shaktipat' refers to an experience people report as receiving a direct download, energy or insight from another person, often through a simple gaze or touch.

Years later in a tiny book nook hidden on the bank of the Animus River in Durango, CO, the river of lost souls, I encountered his master work on a high shelf in two volumes. The bookseller said, "I was waiting for someone special to come to buy this book." *From the Finite to the Infinite* now graces the round glass coffee table, another mandala, in my living room, along with *Guanyin the Goddess of Compassion*.

Frequently in my passage through life, I have encountered different branches of yoga. I started with training in Hatha Yoga including the Integral Yoga Institute in NYC, progressed through Iyengar Yoga, and practiced restorative yoga, with props, in a beautiful studio in Durango, Colorado. I recommitted to my own Wellness Center in Bokeelia, Florida where my friend Jaime was offering Zoom Yoga during the pandemic. The yoga asanas as a physical practice have increased my strength and flexibility and taught me to relax in any given state. Beyond this, the eight limbs of Yoga from the Maharishi Patanjali, who wrote the Yoga Sutras around 400 CE, are signposts to a way of life. Where you sit literally means 'asana'. The virtues of a worthy life are promulgated as aspiration for the practitioner.

Virtues learned through Yoga Gratitude

Open-mindedness
Positive self-concept; immortal soul, radiant self
Perceptive self-correction
Profound self-confidence
Playful self-contentment
Devotional character
Proficiency in conflict resolution
Powerful self-control

The Goals in Life: *Purusartha*

Dharma: righteousness and moral values
Artha: prosperity and economic values
Kamma: pleasure and psychological values
Moksha: liberation and spiritual values

Yamas and Niyamas

Ahimsa	Non-violence
Satya	Truthfulness
Acharya	Non-coveting
Brahmacharya	Restraint/ Faithfulness
Kshma	Releasing time

Dhriti	Steadfastness
Daya	Compassion
Arjava	Honesty
Mithra	Moderation
Shaucha	Purity

The deepest beliefs are the Atman or the eternal soul and reincarnation. As my spiritual adviser Sheilana Massey, now 85 and living in assisted living in Cape Coral, Florida taught me; 'We are powerful spirits who chose to come here to have all the experiences we are having in order to evolve our eternal soul, the Atman.'

At the Brooklyn Academy of Music, I perched on a wooden slat and watched the entire *Mahabharata* played out in two days on a small stage. I remember the dice game. The Pandavas and Kauravas are warring. Yudhishthira puts his entire kingdom, and his wife and sons on the line, not realizing that Shukuma, who represents his addiction to the game of dice, was intervening for him to lose. The moral of this story relates to the addiction of pleasure, which is attributed to the battlefield where the senses and the higher Truth fight for the Self.

The Vedic literature, which was written in the Sanskrit language, has also been influential for my cohort. The triumvirate is Brahma, Shiva, and Vishnu, who dreams the worlds.

The Mahabharata and the Ramayana are the two great Ancient Indian Epics. *The* Ramayana, sometimes called the fifth Veda, written in Sanskrit between 400 and 200 BC, glorifies the God Rama, the sixth incarnation of Vishnu, and establishes a powerful moral tradition. The *Mahabharata* (400 to 100 BC), written as a collaboration between Veda Vyasa and the Lord Ganesh, is perhaps the longest poem ever written. Included in the epic of the *Mahabharata* is the *Bhagavad-Gita*, the description of the Kurukestra war believed to have happened in the 9th Century BC. Documented in the Gupta period in 400 BC, the Princes are the warring brothers, Kauravas and Pandavas. The God is Krishna, the seventh avatar of Vishnu. The emphasis is devotion and moral values.

From the Gita:

Arjuna is conversing with Krishna about his reluctance to kill his cousins on the battlefield.

'Thereupon the Lord, with a gracious smile, addressed Arjuna who was much depressed in the midst between the two armies.

Lord Krishna said, 'Why grieve for those for whom no grief is due and yet profess wisdom. The wise grieve neither for the dead or for the living.

There was never a time when I was not, nor thou, nor these princes were not; there will never be a time when we shall cease to be.

As the soul experiences in this body, infancy, youth and old age, so finally it passes into another. The wise have no delusion about this.

Those external relations which bring cold and heat, pain and happiness, they come and go; they are not permanent. Endure them bravely, o prince.

The hero whose soul is unmoved by circumstance, who accepts pleasure and pain with equanimity, only he is fit for immortality.

That which is not shall never be; that which is shall never cease to be. To the wise, these truths are self-evident.

The Spirit which pervades all that we see is imperishable. Nothing can destroy the spirit. The material bodies which this eternal, indestructible, immeasurable spirit inhabits are all finite.

The spirit was not born, it will never die, nor once having been can it ever cease to be; unborn, eternal, ever-enduring, yet most ancient, the spirit dies not when the body is dead. He who knows the spirit as indestructible, immortal, unborn, always the same, how should he kill or cause to be killed.

As a man discards his threadbare robes and puts on new, so the spirit throws off its worn-out bodies and takes fresh ones. Even if thou thinkest of spirit as constantly being born, constantly dying, even then, o mighty man, though still has no cause to grieve, for death is as sure for that which is born as birth is for that which is dead. Therefore, grieve not for what is inevitable.'

Hinduism's greatest gifts to my development are the Truth of Reincarnation and a belief in Karmic accumulation in the Causal Body to transmit to the next life. The old Christian paradigm sentenced my soul forever to Hell for the sins I have committed. I now know that the dualism of good and bad, the good twin and the bad twin, is not True. Sin is only ignorance. *The Dissident Daughter* by Sue Monk Kidd, once an editor of the Christian magazine Guideposts, broke that belief system for me. She left the Christian Church because she could no longer endure a man in a black robe talking down to her from a pulpit about how sinful she is.

The Universal Intelligence, the Self, the Eternal Light of Consciousness has called me from deep in my being when I was sound asleep in Maya, illusion. Vasana is mental compulsion that keeps us in ignorance. There is no sin; forgive your vulnerability and self-ignorance and finish with self-love.

Sadhana, spiritual discipline maintained over time:

1. *Viveca* discernment, choosing thoughts
2. *Vairagyam* stepping away from unreality, achieving authenticity

   A. *Shama* mind management, neutral observer
   B. *Dama* conscious choice to direct senses, disconnect from false friends, pure food and recreation, solitude, healthy relationships
   C. *Uparama* worldly responsibilities
   D. *Titiksha* endurance
   E. *Shradda* trust in chosen teachers
   F. *Samatvan* living by dharma; yanas and niyamas

Deepak Chopra, a pioneer in merging medicine and spirituality, a Hindu who espouses the Vedic traditions, has been there with me on this path. I recently heard him interview Rupert Sheldrake, a consummate biologist who has broken through the old forms. Sheldrake has posited that morphic resonance fields exist as memory forms and bring form into manifestation through attractors. They reflect a higher level of organization composed of fields of possibilities.

Deepak asked him whether this system was consistent with the Vedic top-down system of belief in which consciousness infuses the causal realm where memory and karma live, then down through the subtle body of the mind, intellect and ego, then through energy into physical form. Rupert responded that his view of creation is both top down and bottom up. The unconscious and the supra-conscious meet in both habitual repetition and creative inspiration. Our view of genetics in which DNA transmits information is being challenged by the idea that morphic fields are responsible for forms replicating.

Most recently I have ascended to a new integration of spirituality and unified physics through the Scientific and Medical Network and the Resonance Science Foundation. The old-world view imparted through parenting, religion, science, philosophy and the free market has produced so-called facts, values, and beliefs that are essentially not True. I have learned to listen to my own heart, my own intuitive and inner voice, to cultivate my own garden of beliefs, to choose better mentors, and to engage in spiritual reading and practice. I am ascending out of the old paradigm into the new.

The two world views of Newtonian physics and unified physics are illustrative of this shift into a powerful new paradigm.

Disconnected World View	Connected World View
Man as machine	Fractal and holographic
Reductionist	Whole is greater than the sum of parts; synergy; infinite expansion
Random	Planned feedback and feedforward loops; implicate order
Matter inorganic	Matter infused with intelligence; dynamic
Space as empty vacuum	Unbroken universe flowing constantly
Entropy dissolution	Balance of order, negentropy and chaos entropy

Scarce resources	Abundance
Dominance and violence	Harmony
Brains produce consciousness	Consciousness as the primary organizing principle, unbroken, eternal.
Closed system	Open system
Time and space	Space/time curvature as possibilities; resonance connections
Anti-religion	Vedic

David Bohm, ostracized from the scientific community for his creative brilliance, posited an unbroken universe with an indivisible process that links All. From quantum physics he extrapolated that a low temperature current flows indefinitely through the universe as superconductivity. Nonlocality and entanglement of electrons and other subatomic particles is proof that instantaneous communication across space and time is possible. Another example of this interconnectedness is demonstrated by wave/particle duality, which shifts when the observer shifts position. This implicit order has memory and folds back from the explicit order that Sheldrake believes creates this open system.

HeartMath from Stanford University collaborated with the Princeton Global Consciousness Project to detect that a strong heart-generated collective emotion has a measurable impact on the earth's geomagnetic field. This phenomenon is known as global coherence. The heart has a strong magnetic field that extends five to eight feet beyond the body, thus the Shen in Tao, that exudes five thousand times more electro-magnetism than the brain. In Theosophy and Hinduism, the Buddhi, the divine soul, lives within the heart and communicates with the divine Brahma, holding a summarized form or fractal of all the macrocosm.

The Vedas also promoted the doctrine of World Ages around 1500 BC; in this belief system the cycle is 5125 years long before a new world age begins. Four Yugas constitute one cycle; Satya is Gold, Treta is Silver, Dvapara is Bronze, and Kali is Iron (Greg Braden in *Fractal Time*.) The last beginning was 3114 BC, and so Earth was due for another cycle to begin on 12/21/2012, perhaps the shift from Pisces to Aquarius.

We have much more to learn from Hinduism. One of my next commitments is the study of Ayurveda with an Indian Doctor living in Chicago. Synchronistically, others in my circle are also finding this Vedic path. The path is four-fold and requires a lifetime of study and practice:

1. Learning to listen to the larger self, the eternal light of consciousness.

2. Contemplating and noticing your own thought structure, being willing to change and move away from fear.

3. Releasing from the karmic matrix by converting repetition into liberation.

4. Meeting the Atman (the eternal soul within the heart), no boundaries, no limitations.

Tibetan Buddhism

I had no concept of the Bardo, the Tibetan Journey of Natural Liberation, that is the space between physical death and reincarnation. If so, I would have prayed for the safe passage of Malinda's soul, advising her to avoid the terrible and seductive, the vague forms and shrouded light. In that split second in which the soul can achieve full enlightenment, the light is bright and the path straight. Let go. Be curious. Fear not.

What goes forward after the body dies? The indestructible drop of the energy-mind, indivisible, of clear light transparency, the most subtle essential state of an individual, the finest, most sensitive intelligence and alive energy in the universe, the soul, the Buddha nature which requires the full realization of emptiness, void, or selflessness. The ability to cease identifying with objects, thought, and emotion, a profound relief at unburdening oneself of worry and attachment to the inconsequential. Consciousness, engaged awareness, which passes through Bardo to enlightenment or reincarnation. Often one desires to reincarnate as a human being so that one can apprehend the dharma and ascend toward nirvana. The subtle body with its channel and wheels of energy chakras is liberated to flow naturally in the Tao.

In 2014, I heard another calling towards Tara Mandala. Buddhism had occupied my spiritual imagination for almost a decade, and Lama Tsultrim Allione at Tara Mandala Buddhist Retreat Center had become my spiritual leader. I had studied Chod, a practice developed by Machig Labdron, a Buddha from the 11th century from whom Lama Tsultrim emanated. I was also certified in Feeding Your Demons, a practice with Jungian overtones that allows practitioners to dissipate neurotic complexes, and phobias, otherwise known as demons in the Tibetan Buddhist traditions.

I immediately enrolled in a class, taught by Tsultrim herself, entitled Feeding Your Demons. This practice, for which I ultimately became certified after extensive training and a hundred demon feedings, is based upon the idea of feeding ourselves to autonomous complexes that have taken up refuge within the energy body. If we resist them, they become stronger, so we feed them what they need so they can leave the arena. I still use this practice extensively in my psychotherapy and associate it closely with Jungian methods that embrace the shadow.

The powerful practice Chod originated with a female buddha Machig Labdrom, devoted to healing in the 11th Century. This song allows us to face fear, confront death, and expel demons and illnesses as Machig once experienced in ancient cemeteries. It calls upon all beings to gather for a great feast during which we feed them our bodies as nectar in a great cauldron. Machig offers herself; there is no one to attack; she resists fear, and the demons become her allies. I still possess the transmission of this practice sung by Tsultrim and David before his sudden death.

She and her husband David Petit had built this center from the ground up and were still focused on the dormitory and the Temple. At this stage, the accommodations included yurts, a main hall, and tent camping. I awakened and embraced the three Higher Trainings: Ethical discipline - right speech, right actions, right livelihood; Meditative stabilization - right effort, right mindfulness, samadhi and Wisdom - right view, right thought. Each has its own mind-stream.

My final return to Tara Mandala was devoted to the three Yanas: Sutrayana, the teachings of the Buddha, Mahayana the middle way or second turning of the wheel in which we incorporate the deity, and Vajrayana the Buddhist form widely practiced today in which we are the deity.

In Dzogchen the practitioner goes beyond effort. There is no deity, no path, no fruit; all is already perfect. In the Tantra, every thought or idea originates in sound and is manifested as patterns of light, giving a sense of solid form to the phenomenal word. Five prerequisites for the Tantra: recognition of suffering, immanence of death, experience of compassion, understanding of emptiness, and melting obstructions into the clear light.

The mandala of the five Buddhas itself is an emanation of sound and light.

All is projection and illusion; we are living in a dream. All appearances are radiation from the ground of being. The play of phenomena and the ground are inseparable. Follow the path that takes us out of samsara, the endless cycle of existence. Release the ego from its cravings and identifications.

Empty oneself of doctrines and knowledge.

The mandala principle embodies the five Buddha families who carry the Wisdoms as well as the emotions that cause us suffering. We identify with each Buddha family as we move around the mandala, recognizing the Wisdoms. Then we become the Buddha.

Vadra: The White Buddha in the Center represents the Wisdom of Basic Space; consciousness expands, clear light, reality perfected, wisdom. The alternative is depression, identification, permanence, emotional gateways into delusion.

Vajra: the Blue Buddha to the East represents Mirror-like Wisdom, sharpness, clarity; the mind is like a mirror where insults or praise pass in front. The alternative is anger and hate.

Ratna: The Yellow Buddha in the West represents the Wisdom of Equanimity, Oneness with All. The alternative is pride or inferiority.

Padma: The Red Buddha in the South represents the Wisdom of Discriminating Awareness. The alternative is wanting, push and pull, attachment.

Karma: The Green Buddha in the North represents the Wisdom of All Accomplished Actions; all is complete as it is; energy without pressure. Action. The alternative is envy, jealousy, paranoia.

The nature of mind is a vast, natural expanse. Rest in the awareness of the vastness of the Great Mind Stream. It is a cognition without duality. For direct liberation from mind, turn directly to a thought, or a pain or an emotion, and it liberates itself. Look at it, and it leaves. Rest in the stillness. Karma is a river of habitual tendencies; liberation is interrupting the karmic stream.

The Three Jewels:

> *Buddha*: the teacher, the radiant vast loving nature within all.
>
> *Dharma*: the teaching, which we can only apprehend when we have attained a precious human life per the Dalai Lama.
>
> *Sangha*: the community, the cloistered life for the monks and nuns, the larger community for the householders who have chosen a more complex life.

The three characteristics of all things:

Annica: impermanence
Duka: suffering
Anatta: non-self

These poisons are the cause of all suffering. The three poisons: attachment/desire, aversion, ignorance/denial.

The virtues:
Meta: is loving kindness for the good of all beings.
Caruna is empathy for suffering,
Mudita is pleasure from delighting in the well-being of others.
Opena is equanimity of mind undisturbed.

The eight-fold path from the Buddha's teachings: Prana, or wisdom, is right view and right resolve; Sila or morality is right speech, right conduct, right livelihood and right effort; Samadhi is mindfulness, calm abiding and meditation.

The eight pillars of joy according to the Dalai Lama and the Archbishop of South Africa, Desmond Tutu. This modern interpretation of the path to joy in daily life deserves a place in the dharma.

Mind training:

Perspective/point of view/reframing
Humility
Humor
Acceptance

Heart training:

Forgiveness including oneself
Generosity
Compassion
Gratitude

Numanakaya is Maya, introjection of the object, assimilation of the illusion of the physical plane, psychological conformity, the shadow, the emotional charge, identification with the object and with autonomous systems such as devils and gods. All of this must reincarnate.

Sambhogakaya is a higher frequency manifested by the Bodhisattva, the Buddha who commits to return to earth until all suffering is alleviated. This is the birth of the subtle causal body. We rise above the object, achieve a transcendent function, and attract an inner partner, projecting fathers and husbands. All phenomena are inseparable; no duality, no concept established. Emptiness and radiance like the sky. Unceasing, primordial purity, spontaneous play.

Dharmakaya is the divine body of truth, pure white light, the bliss body, the causal body in Theosophy that carries the karma. The ego is defeated and must let go. The Self takes charges and aligns with guidance. We await patiently for transformation or transmigration. We have awareness of divinity, the Samadhi. The diamond body.

Prajna Paramita is the mother of all Buddhas; form is void and void is form; Wisdom and Sophia

Rig-pa is skylight mind, void, illumination, emptiness, indescribable, the unobstructed universe, no time, no space, no matter.

Shenpa is clinging, the cause of all suffering.

Clinging: the Source of All Suffering

1/22/18 At a party. Gay and straight in the dream. I stole the jewelry that the man had made for the other. I carried the box with the gold and diamond jewelry by accident from the house. We were at a spiritual school for a big presentation. I went to the second level, but I kept thinking I would fall off. I was in a large round amphitheater. There was a break in the fence edge. We were sitting on a bench of rocks. Rudolf Steiner came out. How were we going to help the world? I crawled back to the upstairs exit and started back to the main entrance. This gal and I were running. I was faster and I said, 'Run with your feet straight.' Then I was flying like I was swimming in the air. People down below were fascinated. Then I realized that I had lost the box with the jewelry on the way. We searched all the way back and saw some sparkling rocks but no jewelry. The guys came back for me annoyed. Where were you? I rode down in the elevator with a gay guy. He was kissing me. Then we were walking back, and I saw my own jewelry all over the sidewalk. Why had no one taken it? Had I brought that box by accident? Beautiful ceramics, gold pins of gods beaded, lying all over the ground. I was deciding what I wanted. I felt hurried and guilty. No one knew it was mine. The gay man went back in the building, presumably to report the loss. I was frantically grabbing and finding more and more. How much could I retrieve? I wanted more and more.

Then I started back through New York City. I wanted to get home with my booty on the ferry. I was going through malls. Two gals said, "Come this way." We were high over the City and I could see the Hudson River in the distance. They wanted me to climb down a high tower with hand holds. I declined and went back in the elevators again. I saw a man following me on the street. I dashed into a restaurant with a gal and asked her to hide me. There was a sleeve on a corner pillar, and I squeezed inside to let the man pass. My old, quilted purse with the Afghan war scene was overflowing with art and jewelry.

Dream: I got Social Security to come to my office and help someone. We spilled ashes of an ancient war burial. I promised I would pick it up from the rug. A man came who wanted them. I tried to evade him. He got a paper saying he could take them. He was aggressive and grasping.

Note: I am always looking for the sacred. I am seeking the ashes of the dead to tell their stories.

Eckhart Tolle differentiates between object consciousness, concerned with conceptual thought, and space consciousness, which is direct experience of phenomena without thought. One only experiences this state in the present, the NOW. He asks, 'Am I arguing with what is?' Surrender, come into alignment with the present moment. There is no point of arrival reflected as safety, achievement or connection. Welcome the challenges, no resistance, no anticipation, no regrets. If we cling to the ego-body and try to defend its boundaries, we will never have safety because there will always be something to defend. This search for a safe place is a waste of energy; the fear of death pervades our psyches. Face death with curiosity. Let go, and safety will find you.

This open space, void, emptiness, great mind stream, great sky-like mind in Buddhism is where I hope to transcend the Bardo. If I pick the bright light, perhaps I will find Malinda still. I believe with my whole soul that I will find her and recognize her.

Dreams of Wholeness

07/03/08 It was an imaginary world. Very dark, a play was going on. I fell in love with a young man. He did not love me. I was dark and alone, unattractive, out of place. Then we became immature people, happy, safe. There were vegetables on the lane. We took them in little wagons. The young man loved me, and the world was good. The sun shone. We went to a place with big rooms. A giant was helping us.

Comment: I regress to childhood

8/3/08 We were an elite crew, tested for cognitive ability and capable of the type of charm and grace needed with upper echelon power people. The supervisor was a man I knew, debonair. We were getting organized and trained. He was a very permissive supervisor. I had beautiful clothes. Power people came and I won them over with intimacy and intelligence. He was trusting in me.

12/19/10 I had joined a very elite agency of excellent psychotherapists. I was extremely fortunate to be there, almost like a spiritual community. I was showing them a film of Colorado, and the house was extremely beautiful.

Huge, three stories, lots of windows. The movie was excellent – they were awestruck. We played it twice. The female executive director was kind to me. Somehow Bob as a young man was there on a bus reminding me of how we did the movie. Hank was in the movie. The sights and sounds were exceptionally beautiful. Then suddenly I saw Malinda in the movie. 'There is Mindy!' I cried. Somehow, I wanted these excellent psychotherapists to know me through the movie. To know my excellence. I was worthy to be one of them.

Note: The movie is my life story.

1/7/11 I was incredibly sad leaving a retreat. I was effectively alone looking to say goodbye. I said, 'I cannot come back because it is too sad to leave.' My friends were impassive. I was thinking of Lake Huron. A huge cove with stupendous waves crashing up on the cliffs. Someone took a picture of the group. I was at the very left end. A woman next to me was kind. The next class was gathered. They were nuns in uniform, head scarves with sacred symbols. I walked inside the tiered hall to see a scarf or rug in the center with symbols. I thought, 'Could I remember or write it down?' Then it was gone.

Note: Seeking the sacred and it evades my grasp.

03/04/11 Caseworkers placing children. Children in braces, playing, sleeping. 'You are going somewhere else.' I could not wake up. I had a paper due but was falling asleep. Another woman was doing it right and telling me what she was doing. OMG. Time is passing. I took one young caseworker on a ride and asked her about herself. I told her I had my doctorate. She was doing her job and was anxious to learn but I was too sleepy to teach her. I just wanted to get coffee and get alert. I had so much to give.

7/15/12 Dream: I am the doer. I was going to become a VISTA volunteer and get the site going. The site was like a campground. I was going to organize programs and have it be abundant and self-sufficient. I was excited about its growth and utility.

08/02/12 At the cottage – another set up. Al was helping me clean up from a music party. Two huge shrimp were shuttling around; I asked, 'What should we do with the shrimp?' I was sweeping. Anne was impassive. They were talking about plans, perhaps music in town. I had women visiting – one was my favorite, perhaps we were lovers. Suddenly they got on a bus and left – Anne, Al and my lover. I was furious, screaming. They came back. I was ripping and tearing and throwing my lover, trying to destroy me/her.

Anne and Al said they did not like me. I got in Al's face screaming, "Admit it, you hate me.' His face transformed to a black mask and he said, 'I hate you.' Feeling betrayed, despairing, despite my best effort. There is a place like Lake Huron with huge waves threatening the shore. My unconscious?

Note: My lover is Malinda, and they took her from me.

3/16/13 I had a little baby. My first and only. Others were looking. I said the labor was not as bad as you say.

3/17/13 I was monitoring an event and came without the official sweatshirt which I realized later. A young woman was angry that I was not doing more. An older woman needed my help. I carried her pills and later brought them to her table after she went through the line. Two children, a boy and girl, making bead designs on their shirts. The designs were sparkly and predominantly green. I admitted them and tucked in a strand for the boy.

Cinnamon, my Irish Setter, went down into a lower area. I was up on the path to direct people. She had a fish. The other animals came one on top of the other: horse, bear, dog. I was worried that the bear would hurt her. Then I saw a small dog on the bear's head and said, 'The bear is tame.' Later children and adults came along and asked, 'Is this the event?' I was telling them, 'Yes, come back. We have started and the children are being monitored.'

06/10/2016 My mother is cleaning a big house for a party. Bob was there, playing with the children on the bed, holding one child. Mother took me into the garden. There were beetles or locusts on a plant. She asked, 'Should I eat this?' She was buying too much, two hams, tons of potatoes, shopping and shopping.

The house had pale yellow carpets and green, yellow, white couches like Harmon Cove. A man painted out of bounds. He painted the rugs. Anne and Al tried to get the paint off. Then two couples came. I showed them around. Bob's mother and father and two friends. They had come a long way and his mother was exhausted. She laid down on the bed. I moved her up and covered her with a blanket. I asked the other couple if they wanted a drink. They were hedgy about alcohol because they were driving. I thought, 'No one else is really coming.'

Comment: The house was mine. I have a dream room, rows and rows of treasures on tables. The treasures are experiences. The house is the self. The paint is persona.

2/11/18 There was a get-together at the hospital and every woman was choosing one woman to invite. I lived in a condo (Harmon Cove) with vast rooms like the soul dreams. I went down in the parking area to a table where they were eating and gathering. They had wine and I drank some. Later they said who drank all the wine. My dog was in the house. I was tipsy. They ostracized me. I went in the house alone and sad. Waiting for Hank. Two men came. One might have been Hank and said you are too obsessed with him and not in touch with reality. Give him up. The women came back and gave me small snacks. They said you can have Father. He was a handsome minister with a beard. He wanted to take me to church, and I was getting ready. Still Tipsy. A chorus of people got together by the pool area and said that I should stay sober. I felt supported but alone in the big house. Lots of beautiful art. I was looking for the room from previous dreams with all the artifacts laid out on the table. There was an empty room with just rugs and lamps. There was a back porch. The women were ultimately trying to help me.

The Return

Once the quest has been completed and the heroine has been welcomed into the higher realms through progressive initiations, she returns as a goddess, perhaps immortal as her Soul is immortal, to bring truth and healing to the communities she has left behind. Some may not recognize her as she is transfigured into a more spiritual energy. Any of this story can relate to the Sole Twin. At 72, I can retire, but NO; am I to take my awakening, my consciousness, my wisdom with me? My mentors have provided so much love and guidance to me; I cannot fail to manifest the same in my legacy to others who suffer and want to prevail into joy.

Furthermore, facing the paradigm of political and social life squarely, I have learned from Foucault, the brilliant anti-structuralist, that power must be deconstructed so that humanity here on earth, through our beloved Gaia, can achieve the Shift. My sister Anne is shouldering her armor on the forefront of this struggle, and so must I in my own way.

The Shift, my source of enumerable trainings and growth spurts, is espousing a worldview built on oneness, not separation. The organization is encouraging all of us to upgrade the Earth's Operating System.

1. Materialism to sacred, living universe

2. Cut-throat capitalism to enlightened entrepreneurship

3. Nationalism to global human family

4. Consumerism to stewardship

5. Rival religions to unitive spirituality

6. Masculine dominance to gender balance

7. Polarization to synthesis (Shift, Vision 2020)

Sigmund Freud, later in life, believed in a Death Wish that propels humanity towards the brink. Both he and Jung lived through two world wars and the unavoidable chaos and destruction that resulted. The opposing forces, Eros (Life) and Death, are influenced by the moral tone of civilization, which at that time was tending towards aggression, destruction and the punishing superego internalized.

Michel Foucault, a neo-existentialist, several decades later theorized that knowledge is a misconstruction based on compromise of our instincts. What are these systems/networks of power? Family, Kinship, Gender and Sexuality, Knowledge and Technology, Population (demography, public health) and Intellectual or the expert savant. We must detach the power of Truth from the form of hegemony (predominance), social, economic, cultural, and military, within which it operates at the present time. The old hierarchical structures and privilege must give way to true equality. 'We hold these truths to be self-evident, that all men are created equal.'

Remembering days gone by

Dennis and I have been invited by my sister Anne and her Canadian-born husband Al to revisit the summer cottage in June of 2018. The cottage has graced the beach of Lake Huron in Southampton since its birth in 1903. The cats are Anais and Simone, seven years old and indoors. One is named after Anais Nin, the diarist and friend of Pablo Picasso. The other is named after another Parisian luminary Simone de Beauvoir, lifelong companion of Jean Paul Sartre and cofounder of Existentialism. Their owner Anne, my baby sister whose quest to achieve has changed the face of International Relations in academia, is a full professor and published author at the University of Cincinnati, teaching Global Gender Politics and Feminist International Politics. She has invited us to the Canadian cottage for a week and graciously hosted us with true Canadian hospitality. Al, her husband, is Ontario-born of Dutch parents who were recruited from Holland to work the turkey farms in Strathroy. Married 45 years and child-free, they pursue their interests with diligence.

I believe that younger siblings of twins are often driven to find power in other ways. Anne allied with Malinda during our thirties. She individuated at a young age, allying ultimately with our mother whom she resembles genetically. She has taken over the Cancer role of maintaining tradition, genealogy, family ties, and retaining her Cincinnati home and Canadian cottage almost exactly as our mother left them. She settled back in Cincinnati to support our parents and did so until they died. Her primary defenses are maternal introjection and intellectualization.

The cottage has evoked a sense of timelessness within my soul. Sitting here on the back porch in the foggy sunshine, I accept that my mother can no longer control me with her voice. This venue reminded me that the rocks and sand are eternal, the seagulls continue to reproduce on Chantry Island, and the lighthouse still stands as a beacon for ships seeking safe harbor in the darkest night. The spirea bushes flower as ever. The cedar trees with their crumbing bark are women who tell me their stories. They are saying, 'Rest here, we will protect you.' Annie has a tiny house where she studies and writes her books in the backyard. There is a hot tub where they heal and luxuriate. The beach with its timeless sand is as the philosopher's stone, stable and yet always changing. New generations of children find stones and tiny driftwoods in the mix. I see my footprints behind me and know that I am incarnate.

Dennis and I walked up to the long dock that used to link Chantry Island with the mainland and allow lighthouse keepers to carry goods across to their isolated home. The water is shallow between the long and short docks. We wandered beyond where the dunes are more extensive. The cottages have grown bigger and bigger with huge windows and tiered porches. The limbs of the cedar are so gentle like wings or ball gowns. I gazed into the water and it was clear, down to the black rocks from the Niagara Escarpment formed by glacial activity. I perceived such radiance in the lake as never before. The sun was flickering on the crystalline water, and I knew that Malinda was there. A flock of seagulls huddled at the water's edge.

Later, I made a shamanic journey of sitting in the shelter of the sand dune where Malinda and I spent our childhood hours. My mind ascended the staircase of the lighthouse to the now electric light, kept climbing through the Milky Way with angels on every stair in white robes with faces of light and seagull's wings into the upper world. The goddess at the pinnacle, also in a white gown, sprouted wings and transmigrated into a white seagull and then a dove; the dove hovered above her and then back and forth from dove to human form. She directed me to ascend and fly. She was evocative of the Native American princess in my Florida home office with the dark eyes and eagle and dove hovering above. Another picture in Colorado, bought in Ontario from the Saugeen Ojibway Nation, depicts a ceremony of Naming in which the woman being named launches a white bird, purified and released, arising from the fire.

The territory of healing is the Lake of Remembrance into Eternity, the huge, unbounded Lake Huron. I went into the water up to my waist, stepping over the glacial stones to the sandbar, and felt the icy fist of her eternal power. Marie Louise Von Franz, my Jungian mentor, in her lectures on Alchemy contrasts the Prima Materia of the stone, which evokes the eternal soul, with the water symbolizing the flow of time and life through space. The paradox is that stone and liquid are one and the same, two aspects of realization of the self. Something firm is born beyond the vicissitudes of life, something taking part in the flow of life, a new restructuring of consciousness. Like the *Shenpa* in Tibetan Buddhism, we do not resist. We do not cling. We keep our hands in the boat. We are dreaming the world into being as Vishnu in order to manifest beauty into form, to honor all beings, to experience joy and laughter. As the Dalai Lama proclaims with gratitude, we have a precious human life!

The spirits have chosen me to be shamanic; I have endured the initiation experiences of suffering and peril. I have awoken to be present to the journey. I now descend into the lower world looking for my power animal. Swimming under the water of Lake Huron as a mermaid, passing all the boulders lodged there for eternity, noting their beautiful colors heightened by their wetness, I arrive at Chantry Island, now a bird sanctuary populated by seagulls raising their young. I ask them 'Are you my power animal, what are your unique teachings, and why are you volunteering to assist me?' Their cries echo my voice. 'We have always been your power animal species; we have taught you to fly; you fed us from your bag of bread, and now we are feeding you with spiritual food.' Their message is "Share Food."

In true shamanic style, I ask myself, 'Are you seeing the world through your own eyes or the eyes of an authority, a belief system, or the collective consciousness within society?' I am seeing through as many points of view as possible: from all positions on the horizontal and vertical planes, through all chakras front and back, through the eyes of my sister Malinda, through the eyes of my clients, through the prism of eternity.

I return to the dunes and a small white plane flies overhead at that exact moment. Is Malinda in that plane? Is her right wing whole again? Is she returning to Lake Huron? I believe in alternate realities. I dismiss linear time, Descartes, Newton, causal forces, the separation of subject and object, even the scientific method. I accept synchronicity with all my soul. I see Truth in that moment. The footsteps of myself and the seagulls on the sandy beach are intertwined. Malinda is carrying me as is Jesus in the poem Desiderata.

Ancestors, sky people, all here today,
hear my heart's song, hear my respect, hear my love,
hear my grateful tears fall.
I am truly blessed.
Max Ehrmann

Last night Malinda was in my dream. I awoke to realize that the bedroom is yellow, that the whole living room is yellow, the center of the earth and the spleen are yellow. My soul is here, the center of myself.

Denouement

Since Malinda's death, my father's ashes have joined her ashes in Lake Huron. At 79 he died of throat cancer which eventually invaded his brain. He wanted to engage in assisted suicide while he was unable to talk or eat, but then one night he came down to the dinner table in the Dayton, Ohio house and announced that he would die naturally. I was summoned to Ohio during his final days in a beautiful hospice room with a garden and bereavement counselors. We sang childhood songs to him and recited memories of him fishing on the Saugeen River and Lake Huron.

My mother eventually retreated into her second family. She funneled my father's wealth elsewhere to ensure that I only received the amount that my father had left me at his death 10 years previously. 10 years of stock market gains disappeared.

The most desperate act of all was my ostracism from the cottage. We had made an agreement when my father died that we would split certain weeks among all of us so that we would see each other. My father, the true owner of the cottage, and Malinda were dead and could not defend my rights there. When I decided to sell my share of the cottage, my mother chose to buy me out with her money. For years I thought that my sisters had used their own money. This expense was the demise of any inheritance I might have received from my mother. She truly believed that she had given the funds to me so that I could buy the Florida house.

My mother died at 91 on April 2, 2011, in a hospice while living at Bethany Village, a massive Lutheran retirement community. When our mother became ill, I had arranged to fly from Florida to see her before her death. My family in Ohio told me in all sincerity that she would be up and walking any day now and transferred to a rehabilitation hospital where I could see her. When I called her room one evening, a nurses' aide told me in no uncertain terms that my mother was not going anywhere and that she had reached her deathbed. By then, it was too late for me to get a flight to Cincinnati, Ohio, and she died in the presence of my niece Olivia while the others were outside talking.

I had spoken to her on the phone, and she forgave me for being an alcoholic. She had projected her shadow on me along with her name Margery. She had also made me the bad twin. I was happy to accept the projection if it took some of her pain away. My sister Anne and Catherine put my mother's ashes in Lake Huron with Malinda's ashes the year she died. I was not invited to participate.

In the memory box that Anne sent me along with some of my mother's ashes, I uncovered two pairs of seal fur moccasins, tiny shoes with red designs and tags stating, 'Souvenir of Southampton.' I was transported to the trading post between the town and the Saugeen Indian reservation where all warm and natural garments lived alongside postcards, wooden pipes, soapstone carvings and porcupine quill baskets.

Suddenly I found myself at the southern tip of Manhattan near Battery Park and the ferry to Staten Island. I was in the Smithsonian Native American museum with my mother. The centerpiece exhibit is concentric circles of hundreds of moccasins all pointed inward as if to say, 'We are all one. We are all headed to the center of the Self which is the eternal soul and light of consciousness. Walk a mile in my shoes.'

Then a tiny birch bark canoe surfaces, also very small, clearly designed for the fantasies of children who want to travel the rivers in their fur moccasins and buckskin clothing, who desire to discover the mysteries of the wild country, who must be raised to follow the river wherever it may lead you, like explorers of the post-modern worlds. I am reminded by the treasures in the box that the journey is all that is. The Native Americans told us, and we would not listen. Flow with the river, listen to the river, the Tao, the way home to the center of your soul.

As Jung intuited, we perambulate the ego in the first part of life seeking identifications and attachments. Then the soul takes center stage, and we release all that to focus on the truth of our eternity. True cessation, defenselessness, acceptance of our karma, detachment from phenomena that do not truly exist. We find our dharma, our true purpose, and express our unique talents for the benefit of all humanity and all sentient beings.

Return to the Tao

I have now completed my Therapeutic Level of Medical Qigong in full and have two more trainings to complete my Masters. When I returned to Dr. Goren for classes at the Therapeutic Level, he opened our powers for distance healing, healing with water, healing with paper, and healing ourselves. We learned incantations to rid persons of spirit possession and other forms of white magic.

Dr. Goren fascinated me with his hands. They fluttered like birds over the supine bodies and transformed stuck Qi into flow. They located and untangled cords between organs and people, purged toxic forces, and tonified with divine white light. I was hypnotized by every movement, every gesture, every beautiful stroke of his fingers.

When the Tao narrowed to Therapeutic Medical Qigong, the power of my own hands as agency, as conduits for energy, as healing forces came to fruition. I had wandered through the dark woods with no hands, as the Handless Maiden myth tells, and then emerged into the golden fruit garden, receiving golden hands as my reward. The *conjuctio* or marriage, the union of opposites, was realized. The maiden married the King and together they ruled the land. The unconscious has become conscious. The latent is manifest. My healing touch was amplified into subtle magical realms.

This power gradient opened memories of other magical hands in my world; hands are great archetypal memories for me. I recalled my father's long fingers and expressive hands that allowed him to hypnotize judges and juries, to play the romantic heroes in Shakespeare and to offer a moving eulogy at Malinda's funeral in his pink pants. My father's hands won him many cases before the National Labor Relations Board. This vision was followed by the small, delicate hands of the surgeons at Mayo Scottsdale and Mayo Jacksonville, who removed the cancerous lump from my right breast and saved my life at 59.

My own hands came into relief again, weeding, and splattered with vitiligo, pigment loss from the calcium deficiency during my mother's pregnancy with twins. My own hands are brown as berries and manifest the white fingers of the vitiligo also. This is caused by a mineral deficiency and is correlated with jumping legs which my mother also had at night, particularly when she was pregnant with Malinda and me, before she discovered the cure of supplemental minerals. My grandmother Margaret Parker Sisson sat at the piano and played show tunes and hymns by ear. I loved to watch her hands travel across the keys. I believed they had their own brains. My mother's hands were also fascinating; they had white spots across them due to vitiligo and the thumb had been dislocated when she was a child and never set properly.

The hand positions of the Buddhas, Mudras, are as various as the shapes of the Buddhas themselves, the Taras, the Dakinis, the Bodhisattvas. Each position symbolizes an attitude, a stance towards the infinite world and the levels of existence. Such unfathomable self-expression and power, the source of industry, effectiveness, and healing. One of my Buddhas holds the Teaching Mudra also known as Turning the Wheel of Law, Dharma Wheel Mudra. Dainichi Nyorai in Japanese. The hand position corresponds to the Historical Buddha's first turning of the Wheel of Law at Deer Park in

Sarnath, India, where Shaka gave his first sermon. This Mudra is formed by the right hand turned outward at the chest thumb and forefinger joined and the left turned towards the chest and below the right hand with thumb and second finger joined. This Mudra symbolizes the destruction of human ills as well as the constant progression of Buddhist doctrines which penetrate to all beings and which without limits like the cosmic wheel exist universally.

During the Coronavirus pandemic, our hands have grown fallow. Will we be able to use them to heal again? Will I be able to open an office again to provide psychotherapy face-to-face and Medical Qigong treatments? In the interim, I can send divine white light to others distantly and be assured of the cure. While hanging the posters of the Tao, created by Mantak Chia, I found myself mirroring the poster of the Thrusting Channels and holding up my arms in the stance of Bringing Down the Heavens. How many hundreds of times had I faced that poster in my treatment room in Florida and mirrored that exact posture without any awareness?

Karma is transmitted by human beings in our intentions, thoughts, feelings, and actions. We are both punished by and rewarded by our desires and actions and by the choices that we make. These vibrations are written in the heart and determine the character that we exhibit. We have responsibilities to become aware of karmic transmissions through the family, the ancestors, past lives, and then to intercept that transmission by accepting our part and making restitution.

In 2018, I faced a bad bout of coughing, perhaps the flu. Was this grief forming in another format? After three days in bed overdosing on Nyquil, I awakened to a new Station as if I were a caterpillar emerging from a chrysalis. Just when the caterpillar thought the world was over, she became a butterfly. My Tao master taught that there are seven stations on the spiritual journey. In retrospect I associate the stations with the chakras gates which we also ascend during life. The stations are permanent levels of consciousness or awareness. We may regress briefly to consolidate, but we return to that level. States on the other hand, are temporary, and we experience changes often.

At this station, I had these revelations: 'Every thought is a prayer.

Every action is a ceremony. Every thought is composite, multi-layered, carrying meanings from eons of time. All time is now. All space is here. Everything is synchronous with other realities. Living the symbolic life is the 'Truth.' Perhaps this is one more deep experience of the third eye opening to miracles, otherwise known as seeing the Truth.

The seven stages of spiritual development:
Reverence and trust
Intercepting karma
Gathering heart and mind; purifying the unconscious
Detachment from worldly affairs
Perfect observation
Intense concentration
Communion with the Tao

Fortunately, every day I find a new potentiality for my life in the Tao stance of Wu Ji, the emptiness between heaven and earth, the Void, the source of all possibility. In Buddhism it is known as the ground of our being, Prajna Paramita, the mother of the Buddhas, wisdom, the source of all manifestation. The whole purpose of life is spiritual evolution, returning to the light, God, the Source. We have highest purposes on Earth that we discover along the path and that usually correlate with loving and serving others. The ultimate goal is rejoining the Oneness, the Wholeness, the transcendent, transfigured Self.

The Tao as interpreted by Dr. Jerry Alan Johnson, the author of our textbooks and Dr. Goren's teacher, provides seven steps of spirituality. These steps have slowly evolved in me:

1. Reverence and trust

2. Intercepting karma

3. Gathering heart and mind and purifying the unconscious

4. Detachment from worldly affairs

5. Perfect observation

6. Intense concentration

7. Communion with the Tao

During this journey, we are rewarded with powers such as observing the present (clairsentience), comprehending the past and observing the future, knowing a person's thoughts (mental telepathy), perceiving a person's destiny (prescience), hearing the universe, and examining the universe at all levels of reality. Are these powers more fully developed in twins? Do we have a head start on the others because of our miracle birth?

The powers the MQG doctor cultivates with practice.

Observing the present clearly, or clairsentience.
Comprehending the past and observing the future.
Knowing a person's thoughts.
Perceiving a person's destiny.
Listening to the sounds of the universe.
Examining the universe and the forces.

The Mountain Home

Hank Walker and I had designed the Durango, CO house together after I retired from the State of NJ in 2000. It was a celebration of our reunion and our future together. The house was built on the Golden Mean, the most common ratio in nature, 1 to 1.618 so the interior felt very natural in the expansive great room. We used Sacred Geometry to honor the space. The house was designed to be passive solar, facing south, with huge windows and tiles on all floors to absorb the sun during the day and release the heat at night, supplemented with radiant floors and gas fireplaces.

Robert Lawlor used Sacred Geometry 'The One-The Divine' and manifested himself within himself to form his own self-created opposite. Three qualities became distinguished: Sat (immobile being), Chit (conscious force), Ananda (bliss). The natural name of a being is the sound produced by the concordant actions of the moving forces that constitute it. He who mentally or physically pronounces the natural name of a being gives existence to the being who bears this name. Sanskrit is the holy language that allowed the house to manifest.

Feng Shui is another science that uses the Tao as its basis. This is the art of location and means Wind and Water. Borrowed from the *Art of War*, the art of location strives to establish the most harmonious flow of the Qi throughout nature. In this system, the green dragon stands at the East awaiting the sunrise; the dragon has intelligence and foresight. The red phoenix with her wings spread guards the South, watching for the noon sun. The white tiger defends the West with her superior and explosive power. The black/blue turtle holds her shell rigid in the North with the snake on her back swiveling her head and viewing all sides. These energies in the four positions and the yellow in the center allow us to properly situate our homes and our possessions within them.

Feng Shui in the Garden

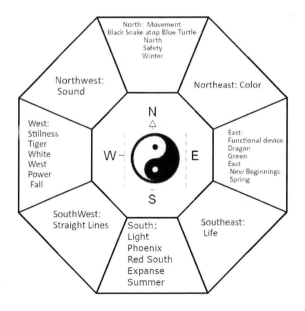

Durango is 6500 feet above sea level, and the house is five miles west of Durango towards Mesa Verde at 7500-feet, surrounded by Ponderosa Pines, Spruce, Pinion and Juniper. Populated by wild turkey, mule deer, Stellar jays, and Albert squirrels, we rejoice in the snow fall, the moonlight and the endless sunlight. The San Juan Mountains loom to the north with more 14,000-foot mountains in this range than all other ranges in the US combined. These forests are a mecca for biking, skiing, snow shoeing, kayaking, mountain climbing and hiking. The Olympians train at this altitude to get more oxygen in their blood. Afraid at first of the vastness, the darkness, and the wildlife, I chose to study Wilderness First Responder, a 10-day program of medical reaction to emergencies in the wilderness when the doctor is not coming. We studied the systems of the body, emergency procedures, and treatment for snake bite, hypothermia, broken bones, and giardia from drinking untreated water. The ski patrol, who witness many accidents on the slopes, took part in our training program. I was ready for anything. I loved to raft down the Animas River with my inner tube. One day a moose walked up the river going the other way. Hank and I worked at Mesa Verde, the ancient home of the Cliff Dwellers, the ancestors of the Puebloans, before drought forced them down to the Rio Grande. I was trained in symbols for Navajo Rugs, Jewelry and Pottery from nearby Indian tribes: Zuni, Hopi, Puebloan, Navajo, Ute.

The frequent dreams of Colorado include a long winding dirt road up a mountain, then a plateau where the house is to be built. Sometimes the house is under construction on an extremely high ridge where vehicles cannot even go. Sometimes the neighborhood is occupied, and we find a small space to put a house and garden. The elevation is consistent. I am ascending to a more beautiful and more spiritual place where the stillness, the natural world, the changing seasons provide an opening for spiritual growth. In the Durango house, I have a dream room filled with treasures from antiquity displayed on long tables.

06/21/2014. I took people up the mountain to the dream house. There were Pinon Pine, a rock and a stream. Many, many rooms filled with valuables, collections everywhere on tables. I was giving it away to Catherine and mother. I went outside and the house still had some land as a buffer but surrounded by busy streets, stores, flea markets. I felt hemmed in. Was it too late to find space?

Dennis and I decided together to return to the Durango house in August of 2020 to rescue and restore it from several years of renters. I saw the house as a mirror of the self: beautifying, clearing toxicity, embracing, expanding.

As I write this book, we are watching the snow fall and collect in the branches of the pines. I am glad that we left the Florida heat and the four acres of natural plantings to those younger gardeners. I enjoyed the Master Gardener program with the University of Florida, and while invested in the huge landscaping project I naturally did not work on the book.

On our drive to the West, we were accompanied by our purebred Weimaraner Sasha, now 15, whom we rescued at one year of age from the Lee County, Florida animal shelter. We realized with horror on our arrival that her back legs had been crippled by the five-day trip. Perhaps she had injured her spine jumping from the truck. She is now stabilized on Prednisone to reduce swelling in her spine and Tramadol for the pain.

The sun invades our beautiful space while I listen on Audible and Sounds True to Pema Chodron, Eckhart Tolle, Aldous Huxley (*The Perennial Philosophy*), the Theosophists, the Scientific and Medical Network on 'Consciousness; Is it primary?' the Unified Science course. Is there joy, ease and lightness in what I am doing? What am I grateful for? What is my purpose? I have questioned every limiting belief and social conditioning. I go to pure potentiality with no resistance, no hesitation, no regrets. I seek joyful memories to break the bond of karmic conditioning. I eschew time and space.

Murray Stein, from Zurich, my favorite Jung trainer who lectures for the Asheville Jungian Society, described this period of darkness with the virus keeping us trapped as Umbra Mundi, the dark shadow over the world. He believes this is the alchemical period of the *Nigredo*, confusion, loss, and despair, which evokes the unconscious. He believes we must move at a wiser pace, allowing more balance and introversion, meditation, prayer, active imagination, mindful centroversion. We seek a kind of Gnosis or knowledge of a symbolic world that contains us in a larger reality. Once again living the Symbolic Life serves us best. In this world, in which we live in the archetypes, and they live in us.

155

The Perfect Life

The Greek philosopher Aristotle wrote extensively on the perfect life.

Predictably, he did not reach any one conclusion about the best life to live. Dr. Daniel Robinson, philosophy professor at Oxford, concluded that both the contemplative and political lives would fit Aristotle's criterion of Eudaimonia, happiness or more accurately fulfillment. If we can find a form of human life in which we do for the sake of pure pleasure, for the sheer cognitive and spiritual excitement aroused in us, and combine that with contemplative devotion of the divine, we have found the balance of creation. This balance respects the beauty and order of the cosmos, and at the same time commits to the rule of justice. This dedication to both the spirit and the polis makes us better human beings and advances the evolution of all sentient beings.

My dear twin Malinda showed us this path. She would often say, 'take time to smell the roses.' She made a difference in the life of every community that welcomed her, particularly through her media and political work in Ithaca, and through her belief in every child she taught. If only I am the Same.

The old saying, 'Life begins at forty,' found new meaning in this tragedy.

Looking back, I can see that my life is divided into two parts, one with Malinda alive and one with her gone. Carl Jung has said that we live the first part of our life circumambulating the ego and the last part circumambulating the soul. We coagulate and then we dissipate. That truth has become my truth. In these 33 years I have been forced to confront the darkest realities, to survive the darkest hours, to truly live the Dark Night of the Soul. The journey has taken me to the depths of Hell more than once and has also led me to the greatest joys of my life. I have found my wholeness on this path and helped many others find their fullness and highest purpose.

Per Clarissa Pinkola Estes, "The one who said nothing good came of this is not yet listening. Those who are in some ways and for some time shorn of belief in life itself - that they ultimately are the one who will come to know best that Eden lies underneath the empty field, that the new seed goes first to the empty and open places - even when the open place is a grieving heart, a tortured mind, or a devastated spirit."

The highest power is an all-embracing receptor who perceives the divine image in us. We must be willing to reconstruct the divine within us, the Atman, and see the Divine Light shining through the mundane. Truly, we must have undergone deconstruction in our lives to be eligible for this process of reconstruction. The Soul Initiation per Bill Plotkin from the Animus Valley Institute takes us through dissolution and dismemberment, then through the Soul encounter where the imagination sees the whole and one's own ecological niche, and then metamorphosis as we embody our fullest identity through enactment of our purpose in the whole. Plotkin believes that most humans have arrested human development in the preadolescent egocentric stages, rather than attaining the adult sense of primary membership in nature, gender, faith, ethnicity and thus the oasis of an ecocentric world. This adultness embodies virtues, responsibilities, non-violence. If we connect with the longing at the cost of everything, we may enter a grief too deep to come out. We must go outside, praise the wild world out loud, and open our hearts and speak.

I have often thought that I would return to France to spend the decade of my 70s. For five years I had corresponded with Claude Denoun, a man I met on craigslist who was trying to sell his farmhouse outside of Paris. Living at the Durango, CO house, I had concluded that Bokeelia, Florida was not crucial to my future and that we could sell that house with no regrets. I had bought it around the time that Hank Walker was suiciding on alcohol in 2006. The years of July of 2015 through June of 2017, Dennis and I were full time in Durango, winters and all. My little three-room, downtown psychotherapy office, above the Bank of Colorado, was a comfortable space to perform Medical Qigong. The friendship with Claude commenced during those years and continued during our sojourn in Florida from 2017 through 2020 while I plotted my final departure.

My desire for a Parisian home blossomed during my visit to France in October of 2018 with my friend Dorothy. I believed that I was destined to be Eloise at the Plaza. We guested with Claude in Ollainville, 30 minutes outside Paris on the train line, and traveled into the City of Lights frequently. Dorothy and I attended the 50th reunion of the Sweet Briar Junior Year Abroad at Reid Hall, toured the Louvre, the Musee d'Orsay, Notre Dame and the Left Bank. I truly understood awe when I encountered an entire room filled with original Van Gogh paintings, toured the Picasso exhibit at the Musee D'Orsay, and inhaled the Greek and Roman sculpture at the Louvre. Our little Renault TwinGo (yes!) transported us across France all the way to Carcassonne. We stopped to visit Dorothy's cousin in the Loire Valley and watched the Vienne and Loire Rivers converge on a sandbar way below our vantage point. I was ready to buy the farmhouse UNTIL I felt the soft breezes and saw the seabirds on our lake in Florida. I choked.

Truly Paris seemed so vast, so massive that I feared my knees would not sustain the walking in the Metro and along the Boulevards. My visions morphed into a small cottage near the Mediterranean with open rooms and soft breezes. My imaginings followed the course of the Aude River and Le Canal du Midi through Carcassonne to Narbonne and Beziers. I was warned of the heavy winds across the lower section of the Occitanie. In this southern enclave known as the Languedoc (language of the South) lived the Cathars who practiced their religion openly until the 1100s. They were slaughtered and burned at the stake by Simone de Monforte and his crusade from Chartres, decimating the south to claim the lands and walled cities of the great nobles. The subsequent Inquisition annihilated them until the Huguenots arose with some semblance of the Cathars. My father's name, Runyan, is suspected to originate from the Huguenots. With the dollar in free fall, I await the time to go.

I am a specification of consciousness in this time and space. I am a symbol of the eternal. I am an intelligible sphere whose center is everywhere and whose perimeter is nowhere. The mandala, the alpha and omega, the beginning and ending are joined.

Now I have come to believe that Malinda is in France. Her spirit is French; her freedom is Paris; her legacy is the Cathars in Languedoc. As soon as France opens after the pandemic lock-down, I am flying there with my friend Ruth to look at all the areas in the Aude, the Herault, then further south in Pyrenees-Orientales nearest the Mediterranean and Spain. I am looking for houses in France in the Aude near Limoux and Quillan. The office building and stilt house in Bokeelia, Florida on Pine Island are going on the market. I have decided that I am finished with Florida and must travel onwards. Pine Island has become claustrophobic.

The goddesses are calling me to explore the ancient Cathar castles in France and reach a new awareness of beauty, life and my higher consciousness. New horizons, a new language, will awaken my mind and heart. This is my center that I must find; this is who I am becoming, the Malinda who was vital and awakened vitality in the world. Somehow this locale is the sacred place for her. I am willing to explore the ancestry on the killing fields of Southern France where the Inquisition murdered the Cathars in the eleventh century and the Catholics murdered the Huguenots in the seventeenth century. These are courageous people who died for their freedom of religion, and I respect this foundation of our democracy.

The heroine gives her life to something bigger than herself. She must die and be reborn. She is ready for her achievement. The powers of life shine through her. The holy grail that she seeks is that which is attained by people who have lived their own lives to the highest spiritual potential of human consciousness. She goes into the belly of the whale, the unconscious; she survives the descent into darkness. Coming into Being is the unfolding, embracing the immortal energy of the universe of which all is manifestation. The AUM. We are all Buddha consciousness; all goddesses are within us.

Now I am writing this book and performing psychotherapy via telehealth in Durango, looking out to my companions, the Ponderosa Pine, the spruce, the pinon, the Stellar Jays, the mule deer, the wild turkey, the San Juan Mountains. I am wondering what best to do with the 30 plus years I have to spend here on Earth before I join the heavenly chorus. What is the perfect life? I have been fortunate enough to be a twin, to be healthy, to have wealth, and to live two separate lives in Paradise. What would life have been with Malinda here? What would she have done if she had lived? Would we have continued to look alike, think alike, love each other? Is she proud of me wherever she is? Is she waiting for me?

As Robert Frost knew, 'Two roads diverged in a single wood, and being one traveler there I stood. I shall be saying this with a sigh, somewhere ages and ages hence, two roads diverged in a wood and I, I took the one less traveled by, and that has made all the difference.' Which twin was truly destined to live and which one to die? We shall never know.

In symbolic terms, Icarus' fate befell Malinda. She believed in the joy of flying. She expected that her life would be successful and long, that she had escaped from whatever prisons had held her and that she was ready to soar, that these friends could be trusted, that the weather was good enough to fly, that she could fly close to the sun.

Om Mane Padme Hum: May the lotus blossom of my heart open up.

Ode to Joy: Hearts unfold like flowers before us.

Last night the full moon shone through the very center of the circular window. Today a white butterfly and hummingbird came directly to me, symbols of spiritual ascension and infinity. I am so grateful for a precious human life.

I Believe, Malinda and I sang in harmony.

I believe for every drop of rain that falls, a flower grows.
I believe that somewhere in the darkest night, a candle glows.
I believe for everyone who goes astray, someone will come to show the way.
I believe, I believe.
I believe above the storm the smallest prayer will still be heard.
I believe that someone in the great somewhere hears every word.
Every-time I hear a newborn baby cry or touch a leaf or see the sky,
Then I know why I believe.

Two weeks ago, Malinda appeared in a dream. She was truly alive and hugged me deeply. I asked her, 'Malinda, why did you leave me?' and she replied, 'I never left you.'

Bibliography

Bailey, Alice A. *The Seven Rays of Life*. (United Kingdom: Lucis Publishing Company, 1995).

Bailey, Alice. *Glamour: A World Problem*. (United Kingdom: Lucis Publishing Company, 1988).

Bailey, Alice. *A Treatise on the Seven Rays: Esoteric psychology*. (United Kingdom: Lucis Publishing Company, 1971).

Beinfield, Harriet, Efrem Korngold, *Between Heaven and Earth: A Guide to Chinese Medicine*, (New York, New York, Random House, 1991)

Bergman, Ingmar. *Through a Glass Darkly*. (United Kingdom: Dramatists Play Service, 2012).

Braden, Greg. *Fractal Time: The secret of 2012 and the new world age*. 2009. (New York City, Hay House, Inc).

Brandt, R.W. *Twin Loss: A book for survivor twins*, (Leo, IN: Twinsworld Publishing CO, 2001).

Brutsche, Paul. Creativity: *Patterns of Creative Imagination as Seen Through Art*. (N.p.: Chiron Publications, 2020).

Burkhardt, Titus. *Alchemy: Science of the Cosmos, Science of the Soul*, trans. William Stoddart (Baltimore, MD: Penguin Books. 1971).

Campbell, Joseph, *The Mythic Image*. (Princeton, New Jersey: Princeton University Press, 1981).

Ceram, C.W. *Gods, Graves & Scholars: The Story of Archaeology*. (United Kingdom: Knopf Doubleday Publishing Group, 2012).

Chogyam, Ngakpa. Rainbow of Liberated Energy. (Dorset, England: Element Books, Inc., 1986).

Chopra, Deepak, *You are the Universe*, (New York, New York: Harmony Books, 2017).

Dispensa, Joe, *How Common People are Becoming Supernatural*. (Carlsbad, California, Hay House 2009).

Ehrmann, Max. The Desiderata of Happiness: A Collection of Philosophical Poems. United States: Crown Publishing Group, 1995. Artress, L. Walking, *A Sacred Path: Rediscovering the Labyrinth as a spiritual tool*. 1995. (New York: Riverhead Books, 1995),.

Eknath Easwaran *The Bhagavad Gita* Trans. Eknath Easwaran (Tomales, California, Nilgiri Press 2007).

Eliade, Mircea. *Images and Symbols: Studies in Religious Symbolism*. (United Kingdom: Princeton University Press, 1991).

Estés, Clarissa Pinkola. *Women Who Run With the Wolves*. (United Kingdom: Random House, 1999).

Foucault, Michel. *The Archaeology of Knowledge*: Translated from the French by A.M. Sheridan Smith. (United States: Pantheon Books, 1972).

Fitzgerald, Robert., Vergilius Maro, Publius. *The Aeneid*. (New York: Vintage Books, 1990).

Foucault, M. Power/Knowledge Selected Interviews and Other Writings, 1972-1977, trans. Colin Gordon, (New York, New York Pantheon Books, 1980).

Franz, Marie-Louise von. *Shadow and Evil in Fairy Tales*. (United Kingdom: Shambhala, 1974).

Franz, Marie-Louise von. *Archetypal Patterns in Fairy Tales*. (Canada: Inner City Books, 1997).

Franz, Marie-Louise von. *Alchemy: An Introduction to the Symbolism and the Psychology.* (Canada: Inner City Books, 1980).

Franz, Marie-Louise von. *The Feminine in Fairy Tales.* (United Kingdom: Shambhala, 1993).

Freud, Sigmund., Hubback, C. J. M. *Beyond the Pleasure Principle.* (Austria: International psycho-analytical Press, 1922).

Freud, Sigmund. *Civilization and its Discontents.* (London: Norton, 2005).
Freud, Sigmund. *On Dreams.* (N.p.: Digireads.com Publishing, 2014).

Freud, Sigmund. *On Creativity and the Unconscious: Papers on the Psychology of Art, Literature, Love, Religion.* (United States: Harper, 1962).

Gibson, Mitchell E. *Signs of Mental Illness.* (United States: Llewellyn Publications, 1998).

Greene, Liz and Sasportas, Howard. *The Development of the Personality: Seminars in psychological astrology.* (London, England: Penguin Group, 1990).

Greene, Liz., Sasportas, Howard. Development of the Personality. (United Kingdom: Arkana, 1990).

Greene, Liz. *The Astrology of Fate.* (United States: Red Wheel Weiser, 1985).

Greer, Jane. *Love Like a Conflagration.* (United States: Lambing Press, 2020).

Greer, Jane. *What About Me? Stop Selfishness from Ruining Your Relationship.* (United States: Sourcebooks, 2010).

Greer, Jane. *The Afterlife Connection: A Therapist Reveals How to Communicate with Departed Loved Ones.* (United States: St. Martin's Publishing Group, 2004).

Greer, Jane. *How Could You Do This to Me? Learning to Trust After Betrayal.* (United Kingdom: Crown, 2011).

Hall, James Albert. *Jungian dream interpretation: a handbook of theory and practice.* (Toronto: Inner City Books, 1983).

Hamilton, E. *Mythology; Timeless tales of gods and heroes*. (New York and Toronto, New American Library, 1942).

Hamilton, E *Mythology*. (Taiwan: Watts, 1942).

Hartmann, E. *Dreams and Nightmares: The origin and meaning of dreams*. (Cambridge, Mass: Perseus Publishing. 2001).

Hawkins, David R. *Power Vs. Force: The Hidden Determinants of Human Behavior*. (United Kingdom: Hay House, Incorporated, 2014).

Hawkins, David R. *The Eye of the I: From Which Nothing Is Hidden*. (United States: Hay House, 2016).

Hawkins, David R. *Reality, Spirituality, and Modern Man*. (United States: Hay House, Incorporated, 2021).

Hill, Elizabeth Anne. *Twin Souls: A Message of Hope for the New Millennium*. (N.p.: Gateway 4 the Golden Age, 2007).

Hillman, James. *Archetypal Psychology: Uniform Edition Vol. 1* (United States: Spring, 2013).

Hillman, James. *The Dream and the Underworld*. (United Kingdom: HarperCollins, 1979).

Hillman, James., Moore, Thomas. *A Blue Fire*. (United Kingdom: HarperCollins, 1991).

Homer, The Iliad And The Odyssey. (United Kingdom: Paul Hamlyn, 1970). Initiates, Three. The Kybalion. N.p.: Lulu Press, Incorporated, 2009.

Jung, Carl Gustav. *Aion: Research Into the Phenomenology of the Self*. (United Kingdom: Routledge, 1989).

Jung, C.G. *Modern Man in Search of a Soul*. (United Kingdom: Taylor & Francis, 2020).

Jung, C.G. *Answer to Job*. (N.p.: Taylor & Francis, 2013).

Jung, Carl Gustav. *Memories, Dreams, Reflections*. (United States: Vintage Books, a division of Random House, 1989).

Jung, C.G. *Dreams*. (United Kingdom: Taylor & Francis, 2014).

Jung, C.G. *Jung on Evil*. (United States: Princeton University Press, 1995). Kahneman, Daniel, *Thinking, Fast and Slow*, (New York, New York, Farrar, Straus and Giroux, 2011).

Khul, Djwhal., Bailey, Alice A. *Death: The Great Adventure: from the Writings of Alice C. Bailey and the Tibetan Master, Djwhal Khul*. (United States: Lucis, 1985).

Kidd, Sue Monk. *The Dance of the Dissident Daughter: A Woman's Journey from Christian Tradition to the Sacred Feminine*. (United States: HarperOne, 2016).

Leeming, David Adams. *The World of Myth: An Anthology*. (United Kingdom: Oxford University Press, 1992).

Mandyczewski, Eusebius., Brahms, Johannes. *German requiem: from the Breitkopf & Härtel complete works edition*. (United States: Dover, 1987).

May, Rollo. *The Courage to Create*. (United Kingdom: W. W. Norton, 1994).

Moss, Robert. *The Boy Who Died and Came Back: Adventures of a Dream Archaeologist in the Multiverse*. (United States: New World Library, 2014).

Moss, Robert. *Active Dreaming: Journeying Beyond Self-Limitation to a Life of Wild Freedom*. (United States: New World Library, 2011).

Moss, Robert. *The Secret History of Dreaming*. (United States: New World Library, 2010).

Murray Stein Ph.D. *The Symbolic Life: A Journal of Archetype and Culture*,) V. 82. New Orleans, Spring Journal, Inc, 2009).

Myers, Edward., Greer, Jane. *Adult Sibling Rivalry: Understanding the Legacy of Childhood*. (United States: Crown Publishers, 1992).

Nietzsche, Friedrich Wilhelm. *Thus spoke Zarathustra*. (United Kingdom: Modern Library, 1995).

Nietzsche, Friedrich. *The Will to Power*. (Germany: Jovian Press, 2018). Patchett, Ann. *BelCanto*. (United States: HarperCollins, 2010).

Pearson, Joseph., Foucault, Michel, *Fearless Speech*, (United States: Zone Books, 2001).

Plato. Great Dialogues of Plato. trans. J. Rouse. (United States: Penguin Publishing Group, 1956).

Rossi, Ernest Lawrence. *The Quantum Experience of Self Reflection and Co-creation*. 3 Ed. (Phoenix, Arizona: Seig Tucker & Theisen Inc. 2000).

Rossi, Safron., Le Grice, Keiron., Jung, C. G. *Jung on Astrology*. (United Kingdom: Taylor & Francis, 2017).

Ruiz, Miguel., Mills, Janet. *The Four Agreements: A Practical Guide to Personal Freedom*, Paperback. (United Kingdom: Amber-Allen Pub., 1997).

Saint-Exupéry, Antoine de. *The Little Prince: And, Letter to a Hostage*. (United Kingdom: Penguin, 2006). Saramago, Jose. The Double.

Sartre, Jean-Paul. *Being and Nothingness*. (United States: Washington Square Press, 1992).

Sasportas, Howard., Greene, Liz. *Dynamics of the Unconscious: Seminars in Psychological Astrology, Vol 2* (United States: Weiser Books, 1988).

Segal, Nancy L. *Twin Mythconceptions: False Beliefs, Fables, and Facts about Twins*. (Netherlands: Elsevier Science, 2017).

Segal, Nancy L., *Entwined lives: twins and what they tell us about human behavior*. (New York: Dutton, 1999).

Segal, Dr. Nancy L., Montoya, Yesika S. *Accidental Brothers: The Story of Twins Exchanged at Birth and the Power of Nature and Nurture.* (United States: St. Martin's Publishing Group, 2018).

Segal, Nancy L. *Indivisible by Two: Lives of Extraordinary Twins.* (United States: Harvard University Press, 2005).

Shamdasani, Sonu, Jung, C.G., Kyburz, Mark. *The Red Book: A Reader's Edition.* (United Kingdom: W. W. Norton, 2012).

Shepard, Ernest H., Hoff, Benjamin. *The Tao of Pooh.* (United Kingdom: Methuen, 1998).

Shunya, Acharya. *Sovereign Self: Claim Your Inner Joy and Freedom with the Empowering Wisdom of the Vedas, Upanishads, and Bhagavad Gita.* (United States: Sounds True, 2020).

Sophocles. *The Three Theban Plays: Antigone; Oedipus the King; Oedipus at Colonus.* (United Kingdom: Penguin Publishing Group, 1984).

Thoreau, Henry David. *WALDEN.* (India: MAPLE Press, 2014).

Tolle, Eckhart. *A New Earth* (Oprah #61). (United Kingdom: Penguin Publishing Group, 2006).

The Upanishads. (India: Penguin Books, 1965).

Virgil, The Aeneid of Virgil. (United Kingdom: Random House Publishing Group, 2003).

Wilhelm, Reich. Trans. *The Secret of the Golden Flower,* Commentary by CG Jung. (Orlando, FL: Harcourt Brace & Co., 1931 and 1962).

Yogananda, Paramahansa. *Autobiography of a Yogi.* (New Zealand: Floating Press, 2009).

Mentors:

Jerry Allen Johnson

Isaac Goren

Lama Tsultrim Allione

Caroline Myss

Eckhart Tolle

Tara Brach

Pema Chodron

Marianne Williamson

Clarissa Pinkola Estes

Michael Newton

Rudolf Steiner

Esther Hicks

Joe Dispensa

Alfred Villoldo

Frederick Nietzsche

Doris Lessing

Sandra Ingerman

Wayne Dyer

Louise Hay

Jane Greer

Nancy Segal

Barbara Klein

Socrates

Aristotle

William Gurjieff

PD Ouspensky

Krishnamurti

Taillard de Chardin

Alfred North Whitehead

Joseph Rael Tiwa

Anais Nin

Printed in the United States
by Baker & Taylor Publisher Services